How the Bible Came to Us

How the Bible Came to Us

Robbie Trent

Illustrated by Don Fields

BROADMAN PRESS · Nashville, Tennessee

© 1964 • BROADMAN PRESS
Nashville, Tennessee
All rights reserved

424–085

Dewey Decimal Number: J220
Library of Congress Catalog Card Number: 64–20238
Printed in the United States of America
10.AL64KSP

Contents

1

A Book About God

Before the Bible, there was God,
And there were people God loved.
Because he loved people,
God reached out to them.

Some people responded.
They came to know God and to trust him.
They taught their children about God,
They told one another about him.

Long ago God's Spirit led good men
To put into written form
Truths they had learned about God.
Their writings are preserved in our Bible.

This book tells about the old, old writings
And how they were collected into one Book,
And at last translated into the English language.
It begins with a story of long ago.

"Halt!"

Quickly the word sped from one camel driver to another, and the long caravan stood still near a low hill.

"We will camp here," Jacob announced. "Here are fresh grass and cool water."

Mothers and daughters climbed down from camels and began to unpack pots and cooking oil.

Fathers and sons drove pegs in the ground and set up tents.

Servants herded the cattle together and milked the goats.

Small children, cramped from sitting long in one position, stretched their legs and rolled on the grass.

Babies, cooled by a gentle breeze, stopped fretting and went to sleep.

Jacob turned to the son who walked close by his side.

"There are stones not far from here," he said. "You may help me to build an altar."

Joseph followed his father a little way from camp, and they began to pile the stones in a heap.

"Why do you build altars wherever you stop?" Joseph asked as he tugged to lift a heavy rock.

"To worship the Lord our God who made the heaven and earth," Jacob answered.

NOTE: *The stories used in this book are based on actual situations mentioned in the Bible. In some cases, conversation and customs have been added for clarification and interest.*

"Tell me about God making the world," Joseph said.

"A long time ago," Jacob began, "there was no earth."

Joseph had heard the story of creation many times, but he listened to every word as his father told it again.

"The Lord God himself spoke to my grandfather Abraham one day," Jacob said when he had finished the story.

"What did God say?" Joseph wanted to know.

"God gave Abraham the promise of many sons," Jacob replied. "He promised to lead him to a land of rich pastures and to make of Abraham's family the beginning of a great tribe."

"That was a long time ago, wasn't it?" Joseph asked.

"Yes," his father agreed, "but the promise of God's blessing was not for Abraham alone. It was also for his sons and his grandsons and for all our tribe. God has a special job for our people to do."

"You can't see God." Young Joseph was thinking out loud now. "How do you know about him?"

"My father first told me of the Lord God," Jacob said slowly. "He trusted God just as his father Abraham had done."

Jacob waited a moment. Then he went on.

"One night, I was all alone in a strange place. I had been greedy and cheated my brother, and I was afraid.

"That night God spoke to me, and I knew he was very near. I was terrified until God put a promise into my heart.

" 'If you will obey me,' God said, 'I will be with you, and will keep you in all places, wherever you go.' "

Jacob looked far away at the glow of the setting sun.

"In gratitude I built an altar and vowed to obey God. That I have tried to do.

"God has kept his promise, my son. Let us thank him that it is a promise for you, too, a promise to all our people who obey him."

The stones were piled high now, and Joseph knelt down by the altar just as his father did. He heard his father thank God for the promise and for his nearness.

Then Joseph and his father returned to camp.

Days later the caravan continued its journey.

At last Jacob and his tribe reached the land of Canaan. They settled there and made homes for their families. And there Joseph saw his father build another altar.

Joseph was older now, and he himself worshiped God as he knelt with his father at that altar. And he remembered God's promise to those who obey him, "I am with you and will keep you in all places wherever you go."

In his heart Joseph vowed to obey God, and the promise seemed his in a very special way.

As Joseph grew older, his father often talked with his son about God.

"God helped me make peace with my brother whom I cheated," Jacob said. "And God gave me a new name. Our tribe is named for me. Because God gave me the name Israel, our people are called Israelites."

Joseph and his father often worked together and talked together, and his father gave him special gifts.

Joseph's older brothers felt left out. They hated him.

Joseph was seventeen years old when his brothers did a terrible thing.

One day, when he was alone, they kidnaped him and sold him to spice merchants who came by on their way to Egypt. There were slave markets in Egypt, and the traders knew they could get a good price for a strong young Israelite.

As the caravan traveled south, young Joseph looked at his strange captors. He was lonely and homesick and frightened. What would happen to him?

Suddenly Joseph remembered that his father had once been afraid in a strange place. He thought of God's promise.

"I am with you and will keep you in all places, wherever you go."

The words kept ringing in his mind as he stood in the slave market in Egypt and heard men bidding for him. He was still thinking of them when he saw the auctioneer's hammer fall and heard the words,

"Sold to Potiphar, captain of the king's guards."

In Potiphar's house, things went well for Joseph for a time. Then someone accused him of doing a wrong thing. He was thrown into prison on a false charge. Yet even there he remembered God's nearness and found that God's promise was true.

For God brought about Joseph's deliverance from prison. Joseph prospered and was made a ruler in Egypt, second in rank only to the Pharaoh himself.

One day Joseph saw his brothers again and told them he had forgiven them. "You did evil," he explained, "but God was working in it for good."

And Joseph learned to know God better and better. He taught his sons and his grandsons about God and his wonderful works.

"God has promised to make the Israelites a great nation," Joseph assured them. "He has promised to be with all who obey him. Be loyal to him, and some day he will bring your children to a land of their own."

Descendants of Joseph grew up hearing stories of the Lord God and his dealings with their people. Some of them trusted God and worshiped him. They shared with their children all they knew about God.

More than a hundred years passed, and a new Pharaoh came to the throne of Egypt, a king who had never heard of Joseph. This ruler made the lives of the Israelite people bitter with hard work. From daylight until dark the men toiled at brickmaking, and day by day, overseers made their work harder. Women lived in fear of their sons' lives, and little children ran when they saw Egyptian soldiers.

Yet, at night when it was dark in the slave huts, some fathers told their children about Joseph who had once been a slave, but whom God had made a ruler in Egypt.

"God has promised to make our tribe great," they said.

Often when boys and girls were afraid, mothers encouraged them by repeating God's promise to all who obey him, "I am with you and will keep you." And sometimes young girls whispered the promise to themselves when they were alone.

"We shall not always be slaves," Israelite boys dared tell each other. "God will keep his promise to make our people great. Some day we shall be free from bondage."

So it was that new generations learned about God. Time after time parents repeated the stories in their homes, and sometimes men talked of them in low voices as they worked together.

In this way, stories that became a part of our Bible made their way down the centuries. For the Spirit of God put it into the hearts of men and women to share their faith.

To mark that old, old trail down which the Bible has traveled to us, you might want to erect milestones to honor certain people and events.

For an inscription for the first milestone, will you think especially of fathers and mothers who told their children about God? You might remember Abraham and Jacob and Joseph who shared their faith.

You could never mention all those long-ago people who knew God and responded to the impulse of his Spirit to share what they learned about him. Perhaps for the inscription on the first milestone you might choose these words:

To mothers and fathers
Of long ago
Who told their children about God
And his wonderful works.

Bible passages used as source materials in this chapter include Genesis 30:22–23; 31:17–18; 33:18–20; 28:10–22; 37; 39; 42–50; Deuteronomy 26. Quotations are from the King James Version, unless otherwise stated.

2

"Write ... in a Book!"

In a slave hut in the land of Egypt, young Moses moved closer to his mother. "Tell me again about Joseph and all he did for our people," he begged.

Mother Jochebed smiled. "You know that story better than I do," she replied. "You tell it to me. But speak softly. Some Egyptian might hear and report us for such talk."

So Moses spoke softly as he repeated his favorite story of another Israelite boy who had once lived in Egypt. He loved that story of Joseph, who had brought his father and all the tribe of Jacob to live there in the land of Goshen.

"Never forget that you are a Hebrew," his mother said when he had finished. "You are a descendant of Jacob. You too are a member of the proud tribe of Israel. To you belongs God's promise of nearness, and of freedom from slavery, and a new homeland. He has given that promise to you and to all our people."

9

Ancient Egyptian scribe with writing materials.

"Freedom!" Moses looked down the road and saw the ovens of the brickyards. Nearby, he could see his father and other Hebrew slaves toiling in the thick mud, mixing mortar for bricks. At night Moses had often watched them creep through the darkness to find straw they could use to make the clay hold together. For no longer did the Egyptians provide straw for brickmaking.

Jochebed, too, saw the brickyards. "Always remember who you are," she cautioned, almost fiercely. "You are a son of Amram, who is a Hebrew and a slave. Never forget the proud history of your people, even—" She hesitated a moment and then went on, "even when you go to the palace to live."

"Do you really think I will live in the palace some day?" Moses asked.

"I am sure of it," his mother replied. And again she reminded her son how the princess had saved his life when he was a baby. The princess had not known that Jochebed was the child's mother and had chosen her as the baby's nurse.

"The princess has adopted you as her own son," Jochebed explained. "Some day she will send for you to live with her in the great palace of Pharaoh. As a member of the royal family, you will ride fast horses and be educated in the palace school. There you will learn to read and to write just as Egyptian princes do."

Again Moses looked down the dusty road. This time, instead of the brick ovens, in his mind he saw himself riding a tall black Egyptian horse, as swift as the wind.

In the days that followed, he thought often of that horse, but it was weeks before he remembered that his mother had also said he would learn to write.

What would it be like, Moses wondered, to be able to draw strange markings as the scribes did? No boy in the slave huts knew how to write, and only a few men, either Hebrew or Egyptian. If he learned to write, maybe he could make picture-stories of the happenings his mother had told him about.

Moses decided to listen carefully and try to remember all his mother said about his people.

Moses was a big boy when the messenger from the princess finally came to the slave hut for him. He almost cried as he told his mother good-by, but he was so excited about living in the palace, that soon the little slave hut seemed almost a dream.

As a son of the princess, Moses learned to ride and had a horse of his very own. He raced far and wide over the Egyptian sands.

Moses learned about writing too. He saw the king's scribes overlap thin slices of papyrus stems and pound them into smooth sheets to write upon. He watched them select slim papyrus stalks and fray the ends into brushes which they called pens. He saw them mix soft gum and fine soot for ink, and get water in small jars for their palettes.

When all was ready, Moses saw the scribes make

strange characters on the papyrus, markings which looked something like the pictures he had seen on signet rings and records of land trades made by his own Israelite people.

Only a few of Moses' own Israelite people knew how to write, and their Hebrew letters were different.

Moses learned both kinds of writing. He watched the scribes glue written sheets of papyrus together into one long strip. They rolled this strip into a scroll and sometimes called it a book.

One day, in the palace school, Moses learned to fray a papyrus reed and make a pen for himself. He mixed ink and filled his own low jar with water. Then he moistened the brushlike pen and dipped it into the water. Carefully he brushed it over the black ink-paste and began to make marks on a sheet of papyrus.

Day after day he practiced. He was a proud boy when he could draw, after his own name, the hieroglyphics that included the pen, the water jar, and the dry ink that made up a scribe's equipment. For use of that symbol meant that Moses had learned to write!

It was harder to learn to cut the strange characters on stone, as the Egyptians so often did. For that work, the scribes chose a sharp tool something like a crude chisel. This, too, Moses learned to use. His arm tired, and the tool made hard places on his hand when he kept pressing it against the stone. The work was difficult and slow, but Moses kept on.

Papyrus plants growing by the Nile.

"The deeper lines do not wear away as quickly as characters scratched with sharp stones such as our ancient scribes used," the teacher explained. "And the work goes a bit faster."

Moses practiced every day, and at last he could make records on stone just as those Egyptian scribes did. He studied a form of astronomy and mathematics and other subjects that Egyptian princes must know. When he became a man, he was so familiar with Egyptian learning and acted so much like a prince, that people thought of him as a member of the royal family of Egypt.

Yet, in his heart, Moses never forgot that he was an Israelite and that his people were slaves. When he heard Hebrew women weeping for their sons who had been taken from them, he thought of his own mother. He remembered that she had made a basket boat to keep him safe. When he gathered papyrus stems down by the river, he thought of his sister who had watched over him in that little basket-boat.

Sometimes, when he rode by the slave huts, Moses smelled the simple stew which Israelite mothers often cooked for their children. He knew many of his people were hungry, and after these rides, it seemed that he could hardly swallow the rich palace food.

Often Moses saw Israelite men cruelly beaten because they did not work as fast as the overseer demanded, and he thought of the lazy life of the Egyptian court.

"It is not fair," he said to himself.

Especially when he was alone at night, Moses remembered bits of Hebrew history from the stories his mother had told him. Sometimes he wondered about the promise of nearness and deliverance which God had given to his people. As he grew to manhood, he kept wondering and thinking.

One day when he was alone, Moses realized that God was speaking to him. "Lead my people out of slavery in Egypt," God said. And he told Moses how to do the job that seemed impossible.

"I will be with you just as I was with Abraham, with Isaac, and with Jacob," God promised Moses. "I will help you know what to say and where to go. I will see to it that Pharaoh allows my people to leave Egypt. I will protect them and provide for them on the long journey to the land which once belonged to their ancestors."

Moses followed God's directions. He led the Hebrew people out of Egypt. And he discovered that God was still keeping his promises. Never once did God fail to provide food and water, to give protection and direction.

Across the Red Sea and into the peninsula of Sinai, Moses led his people on their journey. There the fierce tribe of Amalek attacked them.

Moses knew what to do. He sent Joshua to lead a company against the enemy. Moses himself stood on a hill to encourage the soldiers. High in his hand he held his rod to remind the people of wonders God had done in delivering them from Egypt.

The rod was heavy, and when Moses was tired, two of his men brought a stone for him to sit upon. They held up his aching arms and kept the rod high before the people. For they must know that their deliverance came from God.

When the sun went down, the Amalekites fled, and the people knew that God had given them victory.

Then it was that God gave Moses a new command.

"Make a record of this deliverance I have given you from your enemies," God told Moses. "Write it for a memorial in a book. Tell it in the ears of Joshua and all the people."

"Write . . . in a book!" It was God's first recorded command to write.

Moses was ready.

He took a papyrus roll he had brought from Egypt, and unrolled a long length. He mixed ink just as he had done years before in the palace school. He made a pen like a brush. He began to write. In the language of his people, Moses wrote the story of the victory God had given them.

So began the written history of the Israelites which is a part of our Bible. In the seventeenth chapter of the book of Exodus, you can read in English the story which Moses wrote in Hebrew.

Constantly God directed the Israelites in their migration from Egypt. He gave them large and small rules for everyday living together. He gave Moses Ten Great

Commandments which he was to teach his people.

"It is important for people to know and honor me," God told Moses. "Give them my laws so that they can obey them and learn to know and to worship me."

Moses did so.

The Ten Commandments were written on stone tablets. Yet even stones are sometimes broken, and one day the tablets were broken. Soon afterward Moses knew in his heart that God wanted him to do another special job.

On a mountaintop, he again heard God speaking to him.

You can read that story in the thirty-fourth chapter of the book of Exodus:

> And the Lord said unto Moses, Hew thee two tables of stone like unto the first: and I will write upon these tables the words that were in the first tables, . . .
>
> And he hewed two tables of stone like unto the first; and Moses rose up early in the morning, and went up unto mount Sinai, as the Lord had commanded him, and took in his hand the two tables of stone. . . .
>
> And the Lord said unto Moses, Write thou these words: for after the tenor of these words I have made a covenant with thee and with Israel.
>
> And he was there with the Lord forty days and forty nights; . . . And he wrote upon the tables the words of the covenant, the ten commandments.

When the work was finished, Moses carried the heavy stones down the mountain and read the writing to his people.

"These are the commandments of God," Moses explained as he pointed to the markings on the two stone tablets. "We must obey them. Let us keep the tables of stone safe so that we will never forget God's words to us."

Moses knew that the stones should be saved. When the tabernacle was built, he directed Bezaleel, a skilled craftsman, to make a special golden chest called the ark of the covenant. When the chest was completed, Moses put the two tablets of stone inside, and it was placed in the most honored spot in the tabernacle.

In that golden box the two stone tablets were stored and carried safely to the land of Canaan and were kept for hundreds of years. They were still safe in it when King Solomon built the great Temple in Jerusalem and put the golden box in the holiest place.

In the Smithsonian Institution in Washington, D.C., you can find some ancient fragments of stone which, archaeologists say, resemble the two stones on which the Ten Commandments were written.

When the people disobeyed God and did evil deeds, Moses taught them to seek forgiveness and to worship God.

"I will pray for you," he assured them one day, and he and Joshua went into the tent of meeting which had been set up.

In the camp of the Israelites, the people were silent. Every man stood before the door of his tent and watched

Moses. They saw above the tent of meeting the special cloud which reminded them of God's presence. And at his own tent door, every man worshiped God, as Moses worshiped in the tent.

And again God gave Moses a promise. "My presence shall go with thee, and I will give thee rest," God said.

Moses must have written down that promise in the log of his journey, for you can read it in the book of Exodus in your Bible.

Sometimes Moses sent word to the people to meet him at the foot of the mountain, and he read the commandments to them. As the people listened, they looked up at the bare mountain and remembered that there God had given these commandments for them to live by.

Moses taught them other rules. There was one rule about not disturbing a mother bird on her nest and another about the people washing their clothes and keeping their bodies clean.

Often, when the nights were cool, men must have gathered around a campfire and listened as Moses told them stories.

"A long time ago, there was no earth," one story began.

As the flames flickered in the darkness and died down to glowing coals, the people listened to every word.

"And God saw every thing that he had made, and behold, it was very good."

Moses ended the story, and the people went back to their tents to sleep.

One day Moses wrote a poem and taught his people to sing it. A part of the song said:

> I will publish the name of the Lord: . . .
> His work is perfect: . . .
> Just and right is he.

The people heard these poems and stories so often that they knew them by heart.

At sunset time, they often sat with their children in the shade of the tall mountain and repeated them.

"A long time ago God spoke to your grandfather Abraham and sent him on a long journey," one story began.

Another began, "Once upon a time God gave Jacob a promise."

The children smiled, for they could repeat that promise which they had heard many times, "I am with you and will keep you wherever you go."

Boys and girls remembered stories about God and how he had led their people out of slavery in Egypt and was still providing food for them and protecting them from their enemies.

At night, men often looked up at the stars and talked of God who made light and darkness.

"He made the stars also," they said.

Often men recalled promises God had made to his

people and had already kept. Sometimes they repeated promises they were still trusting God to keep. He had given these promises to them and to their children.

And God put it into the heart of Moses to keep on writing.

He wrote to remind the Israelites to keep feasts and celebrate holidays. "You shall observe the Feast of Weeks," he wrote, "the first fruits of wheat harvest, and the Feast of Ingathering at the year's end."

Moses made a careful record of rules God had given to help his people get along happily with one another.

"Thou shalt not go up and down as a talebearer," Moses wrote, "Thou shalt not hate thy brother. Thou shalt love thy neighbour as thyself."

Moses wrote down some of our most famous Bible stories. He wrote the story of Joseph, and the story of Isaac, who loved peace and refused to fight over a well of water. He wrote about the craftsman named Bezaleel.

> The Lord hath called by name Bezaleel, . . .
> He hath filled him with the spirit of God,
> In wisdom, in understanding, . . .
> And in all manner of workmanship; . . .
> To devise curious works,
> To work in gold, and in silver, and in brass,
> And in the cutting of stones, . . .
> And in carving of wood.

Guided by God, Moses wrote down rules to help his people worship. He even told them how the tabernacle lamps were to be lighted. He wrote of the building of the beautiful special tent as a place of worship. He recorded the benediction which the priests were to use:

The Lord bless thee,
And keep thee:
The Lord make his face shine upon thee,
And be gracious unto thee:
The Lord lift up his countenance upon thee,
And give thee peace.

Even when he was an old man, Moses continued to write. Slowly, with his reed pen, he put the words on sheets of papyrus which were rolled into scrolls and read to the people. Some of the scrolls were carefully kept with the golden chest which held the Commandments on stones.

Joshua, Moses' young assistant, learned to write, both on papyrus and on stone. So did a few other men. They taught the people both orally and by their writings.

Many of the words Moses and these other men wrote have been preserved in our Bible. You may read these stories and songs and rules in books of the Old Testament.

On the long trail of history, down which the Bible has come to us, what inscription would you choose for a milestone in honor of Moses?

You would want to remember his preparation in Egypt, and his years of listening to God.

Perhaps the milestone honoring Moses should bear words like these:

> *To Moses*
> *Who learned to write well*
> *And, at God's command,*
> *Recorded God's laws*
> *And told of his dealings*
> *With his people.*

Bible passages used as source material in this chapter include Acts 7:22; the entire book of Exodus, particularly chapters 1 to 4; 13; 17; 19:1 to 20:26; 33:14; 34; 35:30–33; 37:1–9; 40:1–3; 2 Kings 8; Deuteronomy 22:6–7; 32:1–4; Leviticus 19:16–18; Numbers 6:24.

3

In Honor of Unknown Writers

In Canaan, it was time to finish dividing the land among the tribes.

After Moses' death, Joshua had led the Israelites into the country to which they had been journeying. It had taken years to capture cities and subdue enemies. Now there was peace in most of the land.

Moses had planned some of the division of the land years before, and Joshua followed his plan.

"I must decide about the remainder," Joshua said to himself. "But I must have more information before I can be fair to all the people."

Joshua remembered that more and more of his people were learning to write. Some of them could gather information for him.

He called the heads of the tribes together one day.

"From each tribe, choose three men who can write," he directed. "I have a job for them."

The men were chosen. Soon they stood before Joshua.

To each man Joshua gave a small scroll and a brushlike pen.

"Go up and down the land and write a description of what you see," he directed them. "Seven of the tribes have not yet received their assignments. Keep a record of the cities you see and the kind of land you find. When you return, the division of the land can be completed."

The men obeyed. They wrote careful descriptions of the fields and the cities, of the crops, and the people.

They gave their reports to Joshua, and the land was divided.

Some of the tribes received rich land in the green valleys. Others located on high mountains. Some settled in towns along the rivers; some went to take possession of cities by the sea.

The old, old city of Gezer and its pasturelands went to the Kohathites of the tribe of Levi.

Gezer was one of the oldest cities in all the new country, and the Israelites had much to learn about its people and its customs. They must know the best time to plant seed and cultivate crops.

A thoughtful boy of Gezer asked his father about that one day.

"How do you know when to sow grain?"

"There are two special months for that," his father replied. "The summer sun bakes the soil hard, and we must wait for the first rains of the fall to soften it."

Sure enough, the rains did soften the hard-baked land, and the boy helped his father prepare it for planting.

He scattered some of the seed in the first planting, and some in the second planting which came later.

When the green plants pushed through the soil, he helped to hoe flax and thresh barley.

Then the boy joined with his family in celebrating the feast of the gathering of crops.

Later he helped to prune the grapevines.

When summer came again, he helped to gather the figs, and sometimes ate the juicy ones that were too ripe to be dried and stored.

As he worked, the boy repeated over and over to

The Gezer Calendar.

himself the things his father had told him. The words did not rhyme, but they almost made a sing-song something like the old lines you probably repeated to help you remember how many days each month has, "Thirty days hath September, April, June, and November."

Months, of course, were not named that way until centuries and centuries after the boy of Gezer lived, and he thought of the year mostly as a time of various seasons.

Farmers passed on this agricultural knowledge from generation to generation. Finally someone scratched the sing-song on a stone. Perhaps the schoolboys of Gezer copied it many times.

Archaeologists, in 1908, found a copy of it at Gezer and named it the Gezer Calendar. It is the oldest bit of Hebrew writing yet discovered.

In this calendar the months are mentioned, but not by names. They are indicated by the chief agricultural activities which took place at certain times.

Translated into English, the calendar reads:

His two months are [olive] harvest,
His two months are planting [grain].
His two months are late planting;
His month is hoeing up of flax.
His month is harvest of barley,
His month is harvest and feasting;
His two months are vine-tending.
His month is summer fruit.

The Gezer Calendar is written on a limestone rock about five-eighths of an inch thick. It is four and a half inches high and two and three-eighths inches wide.

An angular hole at the bottom of the stone suggests that it may once have hung from a wall hook—perhaps in a schoolroom.

One man who knows much of old Palestine and its customs has matched our months to the lines of the Gezer Calendar.

He begins by matching September and October to line 1. Match the other months and you can find out when certain crops grew long ago in the land near Gezer.

If you look at a modern geography of Jordan and Israel, you will find that the same crops still grow there.

Some of the Old Testament writers must have known the old sing-song of the harvest calendar.

Their food was cooked with the olive oil, and they rubbed it on their bodies. They ate bread made from crushed barley. They wore coats made of linen from spun fibers of flax. They cultivated vineyards and made wine from the grapes. They joined with their people in feasts and other celebrations. All these men were a part of the life of their day. Along with other Bible writers, they knew much of the geography and customs of the people of their land.

Because these and other busy men took time to write accurately of the country in which they lived, the Bible has often been used as a guidebook to Palestine, even in this twentieth century.

In his book, *The Romance of the Last Crusade,* Vivian Gilbert, a major in the British Army, tells several instances of this. He writes especially of the campaign to deliver Palestine from the Turks.

"We used the Bibles as guide books to Palestine, and remarkably fine ones they turned out to be! It was wonderfully interesting to read the history of all the places we were visiting daily, and men in the ranks were as keen as the officers. It was no uncommon sight to come across cockney soldiers out under the stars when they should have been sleeping, arguing about some incident in the Bible because of a place or event in the day's march that made the biblical pages live again."

At least one military feat was accomplished successfully because of geographical information found in the Bible.

On February 13, 1917, British forces planned to attack Jericho. First they must capture the little village of Mukhmas or Michmash. The name sounded familiar to a major, but he could not quite identify it. That night he remembered where he had seen it.

By the light of a candle he began to read the thirteenth and fourteenth chapters of First Samuel.

In an account of Jonathan leading a surprise attack on the Philistines at Michmash, he found a description of a narrow path through the rocks.

The Bible description told of "a rocky crag on one side and a rocky crag on the other side," and at the top "a half an acre of land, which a yoke of oxen might plow."

The major awakened the brigadier, and together they read the old Bible story again.

Scouts were sent out. They came back and reported that the pass with rocky crags on either side was indeed there, thinly held by Turks. In the moonlight the scouting party had seen a flat piece of ground big enough for a team to plow.

Other plans for approaching Jericho had been made, but they were quickly changed.

In the darkness, one small company of British soldiers crept through the pass and silently overcame the Turkish guards. Passing between the two crags, the soldiers climbed the hillside to the flat piece of ground.

The sleeping Turks awoke and thought they were surrounded by the armies of General Allenby. They fled.

Major Gilbert said: "After thousands of years, the tactics of Saul and Jonathan were repeated with success by a British force."

A long-ago scribe had written carefully about his land. The record had been preserved in the Bible. From it twentieth-century army officers had learned a bit of the geography of Palestine and had found an old path.

Yet no Bible writer was seeking to write about geog-

raphy or history, about customs or military tactics.
Because they and the people they wrote about lived in
actual places and engaged in war, these things were parts
of their stories.

The big story these men wrote was about God and
people's relation to him. It was about people's experiences
with him. It included the religious experiences of the
writers and of other people.

Soldiers and judges, herdsmen and prophets, and
farmers and kings were busy men. Why did they take the
time and trouble to write?

Hundreds of years after the days of Samuel, a New
Testament writer gave a reason. He wrote:

> It was not through any human whim
> That men prophesied of old;
> Men they were,
> But, impelled by the Holy Spirit,
> They spoke the words of God

In the King James Version of your Bible, these writers
are called "holy men of God." Through them, God was
reaching out to people. And they did not work alone, for
the Spirit of God worked with them.

How would you honor the busy men of long ago who
responded to the impulse God put in their hearts to write
words that we find today in our Bible?

Along the Bible trail, you might erect another
marker. The inscription might read:

In honor of unknown writers—
Kings and farmers,
Herdsmen and prophets—
Men busy at many tasks,
Who responded to God's Spirit
And took time
To write of experiences with him.

Bible passages used as source materials in this chapter include Joshua 18; 21:21–22; 1 Samuel 14; 2 Peter 1:20–21, New English Bible [NEB].

4

Poets and Musicians and Diggers of Wells

"Spring up, O well! . . .
The well which the princes dug,
Which the nobles of the people delved,
With the scepter and with their staves."

The slow chant told the people of Bethlehem that men were cleaning out an old well. David heard the song of the well-diggers and smiled. He recognized in it the words which Moses had taught his people to sing long ago when he led them to find water in an ancient well in the desert. Israelite well-diggers had sung that song ever since, and young David knew every word of it.

David knew other songs too. He remembered war songs like that of Deborah.

I, even I, will sing unto the Lord;
I will sing praise to the Lord God of Israel.

34

David recalled a stanza of a song he had heard at a wedding.

> Thou art fairer than the children of men:
> Grace is poured into thy lips:
> Therefore God hath blessed thee for ever.

It seemed to David that there was a song to match every experience of his people.

Often David himself sang the old songs. Sometimes he made up poems and sang them as he plucked the strings of his harp.

"David is the best singer in all Israel," people said. King Saul, too, loved David's music. When he was nerv-

Old well near Bethlehem.

ous and his mind was disturbed, he often asked David to sing and play for him, and David's gentle music calmed him.

For David sang of God and his goodness. One day he sang a song about God's care.

David knew about taking care of things. He himself had cared for his father's flock, and he knew the ways of sheep and of a good shepherd. Alone, in the field, he had realized that God was taking care of him like a shepherd, and he had made a song.

"The Lord is my shepherd," David sang.

He knew that dangers lurked in dark valleys where he led his sheep, and sometimes he had been afraid. Then he remembered that God was near. David sang:

> Yea, though I walk through the valley
> Of the shadow of death,
> I will fear no evil:
> For thou art with me;
> Thy rod and thy staff
> They comfort me.

On and on David sang. He knew that fierce enemies were ready to pounce upon his country, but he closed his song with a stanza of confidence. He sang:

> Surely goodness and mercy shall follow me
> All the days of my life:
> And I will dwell in the house of the Lord
> For ever.

As a young soldier, David took part in skirmishes and defense plans, and sometimes he made poems about these.

More than any other person, David loved Jonathan, the son of King Saul. They worked together and played together. They promised to be friends always.

When Jonathan and his father were killed in battle, David wrote a poem which is considered one of the most beautiful in all literature. You can find it in the first chapter of Second Samuel. Here are some of its lines:

> The bow of Jonathan turned not back,
>   and the sword of Saul returned not empty.
> Saul and Jonathan, beloved and lovely!
>   In life and in death they were not divided;
> they were swifter than eagles,
>   they were stronger than lions. . . .
> How are the mighty fallen
>   in the midst of the battle!

When David became king, he was kept busy fighting and protecting his country. Yet, he took time for music and for poetry. He collected and sang psalms of Moses and of other devout men, and he wrote new songs.

Into his songs David sometimes wove the history of his people and of God's dealings with them. Often he shared the intimate affairs of his own life, his boyhood as a shepherd, his triumphs as a warrior, his hopes for his son.

Sometimes David sang of his own experiences of God's nearness, God's forgiveness, and God's holiness.

Once, when David had greatly wronged another man, he earnestly sought God's forgiveness. And his prayer was a poem. David prayed:

> Have mercy upon me, O God,
> According to thy lovingkindness:
> According unto the multitude of thy tender
>   mercies
> Blot out my transgressions. . . .
> Create in me a clean heart, O God;
> And renew a right spirit within me.

God did forgive David, and the king wrote a poem of thanks for that forgiveness. He wrote:

> I acknowledged my sin unto thee,
> And mine iniquity have I not hid.
> I said, I will confess my transgressions
> Unto the Lord;
> And thou forgavest the iniquity of my sin. . . .
> Many sorrows shall be to the wicked:
> But he that trusteth in the Lord,
> Mercy shall compass him about.

David's praise poem for forgiveness must have been set to music. In the Bible, after one of its stanzas, is the word "Selah." That word, according to some commentators, means that there was a pause in the singing, but that the music kept on playing.

The people treasured David's song in their memories. Often they sang poems which David had written to help them worship God.

One of these David wrote when the ark of the covenant was brought to Jerusalem. For a long time King David had been thinking of the golden chest in which were stored the ancient stones bearing the Ten Commandments of the Law. The old tabernacle where the ark was kept had worn out long ago, so David prepared a new tent and had it set up on the highest hill in the city.

He appointed musicians to "play loudly on musical instruments, on harps and lyres and cymbals, to raise sounds of joy." Special singers were chosen for a great choir. When everything was ready, the king himself led the procession which marched into the city.

Inside the new tent, the priests placed the golden chest containing the Commandments. King David composed a new song to celebrate the occasion. In the sixteenth chapter of First Chronicles, you can read that beautiful song that helped the people worship. It begins:

> O give thanks to the Lord, call on his name,
> make known his deeds among the peoples!

A great choir sang the song, and all the people shouted "Amen," and praised the Lord.

Once again the ark of the covenant rested in the nation's capital as a reminder of God's nearness and his laws. Years later, when David's son Solomon built the great Temple, this ark was carried to the holiest place.

Gone were the pot of manna, Aaron's rod, and even the scrolls which had once rested inside the sacred chest, but safe still were the tablets of stone on which were engraved the Ten Commandments.

Like his father David, King Solomon was interested in poetry and writing and in nature. He "spake of trees, . . . he spake also of beasts, and of fowl, and of creeping things and of fishes."

Solomon collected and put into writing some poems and wise sayings of other men, perhaps many he had heard from his father. And he himself wrote songs and proverbs. The Bible tells of Solomon's writing.

> Because the preacher was wise, . . .
> He . . . sought out, and set in order many proverbs.
> The preacher sought to find out acceptable words:
> And that which was written was upright, even words
>   of truth.
> And God gave Solomon wisdom and understanding
>   exceeding much,
> And largeness of heart, even as the sand that is on
>   the sea shore. . . .
> And he spake three thousand proverbs:
> And his songs were a thousand and five.

Neither David nor Solomon nor any other Hebrew poet wrote in rhyme. They did use rhythmic sentences and word pictures, sound words and repetition just as English poets did thousands of years later. And what they wrote and sang helped their people to have certain feelings just as good poetry always does.

Sometimes these Hebrew poets used an acrostic, beginning the first line or stanza of a poem with the first letter of the Hebrew alphabet; the second line or stanza with the second letter, and so on, until all twenty-two Hebrew letters were used. Psalm 25 is an example of such an arrangement, and so is Psalm 119.

Many Old Testament writers were poets, for more than a third of this division of the Bible is poetry. Only seven of its thirty-nine books contain no poems.

The prophet Habakkuk lived when the armies of the Chaldeans were threatening his nation. He recognized that his people had done evil and brought disaster upon themselves. He warned them both in his sermons and in his writings. They paid no attention to him.

Habakkuk faced the fact that soon fierce armies of the enemy would march through his land. They would destroy it just as they had already destroyed other countries. He trembled to think of the destruction of Judah which was already beginning.

The prophet knew that even the beautiful Temple would be burned and the walls of the capital city battered down. Jerusalem would be left in ruins. Cattle would be destroyed and fields burned.

Habakkuk knew that children and even men and women would cry for food, for no crops would grow in the scorched soil for a long time. Most of his people would be carried captive to a strange land. He realized that he himself could not escape suffering.

Yet Habakkuk knew something else. He knew God!

He thought of God's power and of his goodness, and his heart sang. Habakkuk wrote:

> Although the fig tree shall not blossom,
> Neither shall fruit be in the vines;
> The labour of the olive shall fail,
> And the fields shall yield no meat;
> The flock shall be cut off from the fold,
> And there shall be no herd in the stalls:
> Yet I will rejoice in the Lord,
> I will joy in the God of my salvation.

The prophet Habakkuk dedicated his poem to "the chief singer on my stringed instruments."

Other poets sang about the earth and the sky. They wrote about God who ruled the sun and the moon and the stars.

They sang about the little gifts of God—a bird, a stone, a shady spot on a hot day. They sang about God's everyday care—a night's sleep, a stream of water, a bite of bread.

They also wrote to interpret their own experiences and the experiences of their nation. And always they wrote with a sure knowledge that God is real. They told of his help and of their faith that he would never forsake them.

Many of these ancient songs and poems are preserved in our Bible.

On the dim trail which our Bible has traveled on its way to us, another marker might honor these long-ago men who made music and wrote poetry, who remembered old poems and taught them to their children.

Perhaps on this marker on the Bible trail, you would carve words something like these:

To men sensitive to God and to beauty,
Men skilled in the use of words
And of music,
Who wrote poems and composed songs
Through which God still speaks
To people who seek his truth.

Bible passages used as source materials in this chapter include Numbers 21:17–18, RSV; Judges 5:1–3; Psalms 45:2; 23; 1 Samuel 17:12–15; 18:1–8; 2 Samuel 1:17–27, RSV; Psalms 51; 32; 2 Samuel 6:1–15; 1 Chronicles 16, RSV; Ecclesiastes 12:9–10; 1 Kings 4:29, 32; Habakkuk 2:2; 3:17.

5

A King and a Book

In the courtyard of the king's palace in the city of Jerusalem, a boy moved nearer his teacher.

"Tell me more about David," he begged. "A king must know the history of his people. Even though I am not yet a man, I am Judah's king."

Hilkiah, priest of the Lord God, smiled at the boy. "You know almost as much about David as I do," he said. "You seem to try to be exactly like him."

Young Josiah's face flushed.

"I am proud that King David was a relative of mine," he admitted. "He did much for our people, for he knew and followed the Lord God."

"Indeed David was a good king," Hilkiah replied, "but it was not so with many later kings. They led the country in evil ways. It was because of an unreasonable king that the nation of Israel split into two governments, and you rule only the southern kingdom of Judah."

"That split came about three hundred years ago, didn't it?" Josiah asked.

Hilkiah nodded.

"Yes," he said. "During those years, the people of Judah have forgotten how to be loyal to the Lord God whom their ancestors served. They have set up idols all over the country. They treat one another wickedly. The Temple of the Lord God is almost in ruins."

Josiah looked up the hill. He could see broken stones and fallen timbers. He knew that even inside the Temple, shrines to heathen gods had been set up.

"I will never worship an idol," he vowed to himself. "Some day—"

Josiah did not finish his thought, for again Hilkiah was speaking. "Our country of Judah is only a vassal state, paying taxes to a foreign power.

"Once prophets of the Lord God spoke in this land," Hilkiah continued. "Some of them even recorded their experiences with God. Copies of God's laws were made."

"Who copied them?" Josiah wanted to know.

"Men who had learned to write," Hilkiah replied. "They were called scribes."

"Did other people write?" Josiah asked.

"A few," Hilkiah answered. "King Hezekiah wrote poetry. And some of the prophets wrote. But most that was written has been lost."

Josiah sighed. He knew there were few books in his country.

An old scroll helped a nation find God again.

As Josiah grew older, he learned more about the history of his people, and he learned more about God.

By the time he was twenty years old, he had come to know God for himself. He was also getting rid of idols in his country. He tore down heathen altars in the Temple and wherever they had been set up.

King Josiah also called on his people to worship the Lord God. He ordered the Temple repaired. Work began.

One day Shaphan, secretary to the priest Hilkiah, came running to the palace with a bundle in his hand.

"Hilkiah has sent this to you," Shaphan panted. He pointed to the bundle he had brought.

"As workmen were repairing the Temple, Hilkiah found this book. He says it is the book of the Law of the Lord."

Carefully, Shaphan took the covering from the bundle. He unrolled an old scroll, and read some of its words to the king. They told of the dreadful consequences of failing to honor God.

As he listened, the king began to pace the floor.

"This is indeed the book of the Law of the Lord," he realized. He sent messengers to tell the men of Judah to meet him at the Temple and bring other people with them.

> And the king went up into the house of the Lord,
> And all the men of Judah
> And all the inhabitants of Jerusalem with him,
> And the priest, and the prophets,

And all the people, both small and great:
And he read in their ears all the words
Of the book of the covenant
Which was found in the house of the Lord.

When the reading was finished, the king took his stand by a pillar of the Temple and made a solemn promise to God.

"I promise the Lord God that I will keep these laws he has given," King Josiah said.

"With all his heart and his soul," the king promised to perform the words of the covenant that were written in the old scroll.

As the people of Judah had listened to King Josiah read the book of the Law of God, they remembered worshiping idols. They thought of times they had not been just. They, too, made a covenant with God.

"We, too, will worship God and obey his laws," they promised.

They began to help the king to destroy idols and altars to false gods. They observed the old Passover Feast which God had commanded. They told their children of God's goodness in delivering their ancestors from slavery in Egypt and in bringing them to a new land.

At last Temple repairs were completed, and the people worshiped the Lord God there.

What was the book that brought all this about, the book that was found in the half-ruined Temple at Jerusalem?

Scholars agree that it was a copy of all, or parts of, the book of Deuteronomy, the fifth book in your Bible.

Many of these scholars think that the old scroll contained what we now know as the twenty-eighth, twenty-ninth, and thirtieth chapters of Deuteronomy.

After Josiah's death, the people of Judah, along with their new king, returned to the worship of idols and to wicked living.

What, then, did King Josiah accomplish that was of permanent value?

One thing alone has endured. Because he sought to provide a worthy place for his people to worship God, an old scroll, forgotten through the years, was found. And the words on that scroll still speak to people today from the pages of Deuteronomy.

In that book people can still find laws of God. They can discover fair and just ways of treating each other. They can find warnings.

Yet the book of Deuteronomy is far more than laws and rules and warnings. In this book we can learn about God and his goodness. We can find words that help us to worship God and to be glad for his care.

For the book of Deuteronomy is a record of God's working with men and women of other centuries. It tells how he sought patiently and lovingly, sometimes even sternly, to help his people to know him and to follow his good plans for them.

Today, God still speaks through the experiences of

these men and women who lived long ago. And to those who listen and seek his way, he gives a message of fresh confidence. In the book of Deuteronomy is this assurance,

> The eternal God is thy refuge,
> And underneath are the everlasting arms.

King Josiah, who respected and cherished words of an ancient scroll, has earned a place among those who are honored by markers along the Bible trail.

On the dim path which began centuries ago, there might be erected a bronze tablet in memory of him and others like him. On it you might read a statement something like this:

> *This marker is dedicated*
> *To the memory of King Josiah*
> *And all other persons*
> *Whose work brought about the discovery*
> *Of long-ago records*
> *Written by men inspired of God.*

Bible passages used as source material in this chapter include 2 Kings 22 to 23; 2 Chronicles 34; Deuteronomy 33:27.

6

A Twice-Written Book

Southwest of the city of Jerusalem is a mound of earth, today called Ras-el-Kharrubah. Long ago there was a little village at this place, a village called Anathoth. In this village, in the days of King Josiah, a boy was approaching manhood.

His name was Jeremiah, and he was keenly alert to all that went on about him. He seemed to miss nothing. In the springtime, he sniffed the perfume of budding almond blossoms; later he watched ripe figs brought to the Temple as offerings to God and noticed that some of them were spoiled. He saw harvests of green olives, and shepherds watching their sheep.

Jeremiah was also alert to things he could neither see nor touch. For one day he knew in his heart that God wanted him to do something.

"I have a plan for you," God told Jeremiah. "I want you to speak to the people for me. I want you to be my prophet."

"Me speak for the Lord God!" The idea terrified Jeremiah. "I am too young," he argued. "I can never do that."

"Do not be afraid," God told Jeremiah. "I am with you. I will put my words in your mouth."

Jeremiah needed that assurance. He knew that not all the people of Judah agreed with the reforms King Josiah had brought about. Many of them who agreed did so only with their lips but not in their hearts. Some of them even continued to worship idols.

"Warn the people about the evil things they are doing," God instructed Jeremiah. "Warn them that they will be captured by another nation and carried away to a strange land if they continue in their evil ways."

Jeremiah obeyed. He reminded the people that evil always brings its own punishment and that they could not continue to disobey God and hope for his protection.

Many of the people of Judah resented the words Jeremiah spoke.

After the death of King Josiah, such resentment spread. More and more people returned to wicked ways of living and to the worship of idols. For twenty-five years evil kings reigned in Judah, and, during all those years, Jeremiah spoke warnings just as God directed him.

"Unless we change our ways, our nation will be destroyed," he declared. "Our people will be deported to Babylon.

"There is just one hope for you. God is good. He loves

you and wants to help you. If you will turn from evil and honor him, he will forgive you. He will give you the blessings of peace."

Neither king nor people paid any attention to the prophet. They put him in stocks at the city gate where all the people could see his misery and laugh at him.

Still Jeremiah continued to preach. In addition to warnings, one message was always the same. You can read it today in the book of Jeremiah in your Bible:

> Thus saith the Lord,
> Let not the wise man glory in his wisdom,
> Neither let the mighty man glory in his might,
> Let not the rich man glory in his riches:
> But let him that glorieth glory in this,
> That he understandeth and knoweth me,
> That I am the Lord which exercise loving-
>   kindness,
> Judgment, and righteousness, in the earth:
> For in these things I delight, saith the
>   Lord. . . .
> Execute ye judgment and righteousness, . . .
> And do no wrong. . . .
> O earth, earth, earth,
> Hear the word of the Lord.

The people rejected the warnings of Jeremiah, and conditions in Judah grew worse. Jeremiah was beaten and forbidden to preach. When he disobeyed that command, he was confined to quarters in the prison yard.

The enemies of Judah began to capture large groups of people and deport them to Babylon.

Still Jeremiah continued his warnings. One day he had a new command from God.

"Take a scroll," God directed. "Write all my warnings on it. Try once more to lead the people left here in Judah to listen to me and repent of their wickedness so that I can forgive them and lead them in right ways."

The actual work of writing was hard for Jeremiah. He sought the help of a good scribe, Baruch.

"Write as I dictate the message which God has given me," Jeremiah directed Baruch. And Baruch wrote. Carefully he listened to Jeremiah, and, with his brush, made the words on papyrus. He wrote from right to left, in narrow columns.

For days and days the two men worked.

When the scroll-book was ready, Jeremiah commissioned Baruch to carry it to the Temple and read it to the people who came there.

"I am shut up here in the prison yard," Jeremiah reminded his secretary.

"You take the scroll to the Temple and read it aloud."

Baruch did so.

Word of what was happening reached King Jehoiakim. Quickly he ordered the scroll brought to him.

"The king will be angry," friends warned Baruch. "You and Jeremiah had better hide."

In the palace, the king sat before an open fire of coals

burning in a large brass bowl. A servant brought the scroll and began to read it to him.

As King Jehoiakim listened, he grew angrier and angrier. Suddenly he snatched the scroll from the servant's hand. As fast as he could, he cut out column after column of the writing with his penknife, and threw the bits into the fire.

"Stop," the king's servants begged. But the king kept on. He did not stop until all the scroll was burned.

Of all Jeremiah and Baruch's work, there was nothing left but a pile of ashes.

"Arrest Jeremiah and Baruch," the king shouted. "They shall be punished for such writing."

But no one could find Jeremiah and Baruch.

Some days later God spoke again to Jeremiah.

"Take another scroll and write in it all the words that you put in the first scroll which King Jehoiakim burned."

Jeremiah did not argue. He prepared another roll of papyrus and gave it to Baruch. Again the two men set to work. And Baruch wrote "from the mouth of Jeremiah all the words of the book which Jehoiakim king of Judah had burned in the fire."

At last the scroll was again complete, "and there were added besides unto them many like words."

In the meantime, Jeremiah saw many of his people carried captive to Babylon.

"Write these exiles a letter," God directed him one day. "Tell them this nation of Judah will fall. They must make

the best of their situation. They shall be captives for
seventy years, but I am still seeking to help them. Assure
them that I will hear their prayers even in Babylon when
they seek me with all their hearts. When they do that,
their captivity will end."

Jeremiah wrote the letter and sent it to Babylon. In
spite of discouragements, he kept on speaking for God
both orally and in writing. And he came to realize that it
is not enough for God's laws to be known or even for his
messages to be recorded on papyrus or sheepskin or
stone.

In his book he recorded a great hope, a hope confirmed
by a promise from God.

> Behold, the days come, saith the Lord,
> That I will make a new covenant
> With the house of Israel,
> And with the house of Judah: . . .
> I will put my law in their inward parts,
> And write it in their hearts;
> And will be their God,
> And they shall be my people. . . .
> They shall all know me,
> From the least to the greatest of them,
> Saith the Lord:
> For I will forgive them their iniquity.

At last Judah was completely overcome by her enemies.
When the Temple at Jerusalem was burned in 586 B.C.,

most of the captured people, especially the leaders and more-educated men, were deported to Babylon. A few of the poor were allowed to remain in their own land. Baruch and Jeremiah were sent to Egypt. Baruch must have carried the manuscripts of Jeremiah's book with him to Tahpanhes, near the present site of the Suez Canal, and there he continued to record Hebrew history, along with God's later messages.

In Babylon, the captives from Judah were settled on the fertile banks of the Chebar River. This "river" was really a canal which ran parallel to the Euphrates River. It had been dug to drain the swamps at one season and irrigate them at another. Nearby was the old, old city of Nippur, with its strange jagged-roofed temple built to honor the moon-god.

The river Chebar in Babylon.

Some of the captives from Judah began to follow the customs of their conquerors. They became successful businessmen. Most of them were loyal to their religion.

Others found it difficult to adjust to the new life.

When they ate cakes of bread made from crushed marsh millet, they remembered the barley bread which had tasted so good back in Judah.

When the hot, damp winds blew, they remembered cool breezes from the hills of their own country.

And when they looked at the towers of the temple to the moon-god, in their minds they saw only the ruins of their own Temple on Mount Zion in Jerusalem.

"Sing for us," the Babylonians demanded of these captives. "Sing us lively, cheerful songs of your own land."

The people tried to obey, but there was no music in them, and the words choked in their throats.

One man wrote a poem about that experience.

> By the rivers of Babylon, there we sat down,
> . . . we wept, when we remembered Zion.
> We hanged our harps upon the willows. . . .
>   for there
> They that carried us away captive required of us
>   a song; . . .
> Saying, "Sing us one of the songs of Zion."
> How shall we sing the Lord's song in a strange
>   land?
> If I forget thee, O Jerusalem,
> Let my right hand forget her cunning.

You can find that poem in your Bible. It is Psalm 137.

Yet many of the exiles discovered that they could still worship God, even without a temple. In their homes, they prayed. They told their children stories of King David and other heroes of their history.

"Solomon, who was once our king, was famous all over the world," they said. "He wrote many wise sayings."

Scribes in Babylon collected all the bits of Hebrew writing they could find. They found writings that told of the history of Israel and Judah. They found some scrolls that included parts of sermons prophets had jotted down. They found several songs King David had written and others he had collected.

One special scroll these captives cherished. It was the scroll which had been discovered during the reign of Josiah.

This scroll was wearing out. Ezra and other careful scribes made copies of it. They added other laws and stories they had heard. They added laws from other bits of writing they had found.

Devout exiles began to think more and more about God and his laws. They met together in their homes in small groups and talked about them. They taught them to younger men.

These gatherings in Babylon were, historians think, the beginning of synagogues. "House synagogues," one writer calls them.

In these meetings there was one textbook, the sacred Law. It was explained and often memorized. The history of the Hebrew people was retold and the old scrolls studied. It was natural to worship as God's Law was studied, so synagogue services became worship services also.

And God did not leave his people in Babylon without a religious leader. One of the exiles was the prophet Ezekiel. Now God called him to minister to his people, much as a good pastor might do.

Ezekiel reminded his exiled people of God's standards and of his goodness, of his mercy, of his forgiving love. He comforted them with God's promise that some of their children would return to the land of Judah after long years in Babylon.

Ezekiel was also a writer. Of his messages, he wrote, "Thus saith the Lord."

In Babylon, these exiles from the land of Judah came to be called Jews. And they learned many new things. Many of them learned a language called Aramaic.

A modern writer tells us that Aramaic is as old as Hebrew and that it was the international language of the days of the Babylonian captivity. State documents between countries were often written in it, and it commanded international respect much as the English language does today.

The Jews in Babylon began to think of Aramaic as the everyday language of their people and of Hebrew as the language of literature. They had their scribes copy some of their Scriptures in Aramaic. These copies, so far as we know, were the first translation of a part of the Bible into a new language.

New Scriptures were also written during the time of the captivity, for God continued to work with his people and to comfort them through men who dared speak for him.

God was also using more and more people to record his messages. His Spirit was inspiring more and more men to write.

Along the trail down which the Bible has come to us, a marker might be erected in memory of Jeremiah and Baruch and other courageous men who helped to give us our Bible.

The inscription might read:

In honor of secretaries and prophets,
And other men who obeyed God
And dared speak for him with their mouths
And write for him with their pens.

Bible passages used as source material in this chapter include the book of Jeremiah, especially chapters 9; 29; 31; 36; Psalm 137.

7

More than Half Our Bible

"A new king rules!" Throughout the cities of Babylon, heralds proclaimed the news. The word spread all over the kingdom, even to the Jewish people who lived by the river Chebar.

"Who is the new king?" people asked. "What has happened? What will be done with people like us who have been captured and brought here from other lands?"

"Cyrus of Persia is the new king," was the reply. "The Persians have conquered Babylon."

The exiles from Judah had to wait longer for an answer to their last question.

"King Cyrus is interested in foreigners as well as in the natives of Babylon," a man finally reported one day. "He has issued a proclamation that any Jew who wishes may go back to Judah. He says that the Persian Government will even help us to rebuild our Temple, which was burned when the city of Jerusalem was captured."

Many of these Jewish people had chosen the religion of their ancestors in place of the idol worship of Babylon. They, in turn, had taught their religion to their children and instructed them in the laws of the Lord God. And they were patriots.

In small and larger groups, they began to talk about going back to the land of Judah. Some of them had been babies when they were brought to Babylon. They remembered hearing their mothers sing songs from the old psalms of famous King David. They had grown up hearing tales of Jerusalem and of the Temple. They had learned about the Lord God and his laws. They had watched their parents praying, always turning their faces toward Jerusalem, called the Holy City because the Temple of God had once stood there on the highest hill. They talked about all these things.

"Our countrymen back in Judah need us," one man added. "They are in a pitiful condition."

At last a decision was reached.

"Let us take our families to our old homeland," many men decided. "There we can rear our children among people who believe as we do."

"We can help the people there rebuild our country."

"Perhaps some day we can even build the Temple in Jerusalem again."

Groups of men, women, and children got ready and marched out of Babylon.

"There go some of those Jewish exiles who have lived

here for more than sixty years," the Babylonians observed. "Many of them have never been happy here, for they did not like our customs or our religion."

Ezra, the scribe, led one group of people back to Judah.

Nehemiah, cupbearer to King Cyrus, led another group.

Under the leadership of Zerubbabel, one company of more than 42,000 people returned to Jerusalem.

As these people left the land of their captivity, they carried at least two new ideas which they had not brought with them from Judah.

One of these was a new name—they were called Jews.

Another was a new idea for a house of worship and study—the synagogue.

They also carried something that they could see and touch—new scrolls of the Scriptures. Carefully the scribes had copied old manuscripts. With painstaking care they had formed each letter and word, being careful to clean their brushes each time before they wrote the holy name of God. Other writings had been gathered together and compiled, and new writings had been made.

The Jews had brought part of the Law to Babylon. They took back to Judah the entire book of the Law—the Pentateuch.

When they arrived in Judah, the people sought the native towns of their families. "My father told me about this place," someone would say. And occasionally an old man would add, "I remember it myself."

In these towns and all over Judah the returned exiles found settlements of families of poorer and less-educated Jews who had been left behind when the deportation to Babylon was made. A few of the old men and women were still living.

The returned groups joined the families who had remained. They encouraged these families, and they shared with them.

"We have two big jobs to do," the newly arrived leaders reminded the people of Judah. "The Temple must be rebuilt, and so must the walls of Jerusalem."

In Jerusalem the people gathered one day about the ruins of the Temple. Stone by stone they built a new altar where the old one had been. They worshiped God. Then they made leafy shelters and celebrated the ancient feast of the harvest. Together they made plans to build a new Temple.

When the foundation was laid, the priests blew on trumpets and the choir sang just as they had done years before in the Temple.

The people heard the song, and some of them cried for joy as they recognized the familiar words:

> O give thanks unto the Lord, . . .
> For he is good,
> For his steadfast love endures for
> ever toward Israel.

When service was over, the people returned to their homes. Busy with planting and harvest, working at their oilpresses and the building of houses to live in, they for a time seemed to forget to complete the Temple.

Nehemiah was busy helping workmen rebuild the walls of the city.

The prophet Haggai saw all the work that was going on. He looked at the foundations of the Temple on which nothing had been built.

"Send to the hills and bring cedar wood," he told the people one day. "Get workmen and cut stones. It is time for us to finish building the Temple which we began years ago."

Slowly stones were lifted into place, and again the walls stood. The roof was completed. Carefully, skilled workmen carved wood and lined the inside of the building with it.

At last the Temple was finished.

Leaders in worship were appointed. They studied the scroll of the Law which had been brought back from Babylon, and planned a dedication service. They planned it to be as much as possible like the dedication of the old tabernacle which their ancestors had built hundreds of years before in the wilderness.

In the holy of holies, the most honored spot, they placed the scrolls, the newly copied book of the Law.

From all the towns of Judah the people came to the dedication. They gasped in surprise when they saw in their places the gold and silver vessels which King Artaxerxes had sent back from Babylon.

"We never thought we would see these holy vessels again," an old man said to another. "They were stolen from the old Temple by enemy soldiers and carried to Babylon years ago."

They pointed out the shining cups of silver and gold to their children.

The priests read from God's Law, and the people listened.

The trumpets made joyful music and the choirs sang:

> I was glad when they said unto me,
> Let us go into the house of the Lord.

Together, in the Temple they had rebuilt, the people of Judah worshiped God again.

When the service was over, the people realized that there was much they did not know about the Law.

"Ezra the scribe must teach us," they decided. "He has studied the law of the Lord. He himself lives by it." They sent for Ezra.

The old scribe knew that some of these people had lived so long in Babylon that they had forgotten the Hebrew language. Many boys and girls who had grown up there spoke only Aramaic. The people who had remained in Judah knew only Hebrew. Ezra chose teachers who knew both languages.

One day he carried the book of the Law to a platform built down by the Water Gate in Jerusalem. People crowded around him, men and women and boys and girls.

Ezra showed them the scroll of God's Law, and the people stood up and praised God.

Then Ezra began to read. From early morning until noon Ezra read, speaking clearly, and all the people paid attention to his words.

In words that could be understood, teachers explained what Ezra read. The people listened and learned what God wanted them to do.

"We must learn more about God's laws," they decided.

In communities all over Judah, synagogues were built, wherever there could be found "ten men of leisure" with time to look after their affairs. Word for word, the Law was repeated, and many rules added to it.

Since all the people could not go to the Temple in Jerusalem, these synagogues became places for prayer as well as for the study of the Scriptures. Men attended their services, and later boys, and sometimes women.

Yet Jerusalem and the Temple remained the center of Jewish life, and there scribes continued to work on their writings. Some of them copied faded words from worn scrolls of the Law, and often these copyists interpreted what they wrote, sometimes orally, sometimes by comments added on the manuscripts which they prepared.

Being a scribe became a profession, and many scribes became traveling teachers as well as writers. Professional scribes investigated and studied not only the Scriptures but other books. They advised people and gave lectures and won the respect of the people. One historian says that Ezra organized the scribes of Jerusalem into a guild.

Scribes also began to collect fragments of ancient manuscripts. Carefully they sorted these, and so compiled a collection of books which were included in the Jewish Scriptures.

New scrolls of Scripture were also written, for a few prophets of the Lord both spoke and wrote after the return of the exiles to Judah.

By the close of the last century before Jesus was born, the Scriptures of the Jews contained three divisions:

> The Law
> The Prophets
> The Writings

The materials were the same that we now find in the thirty-nine books of our Old Testament.

Handwritten, the Law made such a large bundle that it was divided into five books:

> Genesis
> Exodus
> Leviticus
> Numbers
> Deuteronomy

The Prophets were composed of what we know as the books of:

Joshua	Amos
Judges	Obadiah
1 Samuel	Jonah
2 Samuel	Micah
1 Kings	Nahum
2 Kings	Habakkuk
Isaiah	Zephaniah
Jeremiah	Haggai
Ezekiel	Zechariah
Hosea	Malachi
Joel	

The Writings included our books of:

Psalms	Song of Solomon
Proverbs	Daniel
Job	Ezra
Ruth	Nehemiah
Esther	1 Chronicles
Ecclesiastes	2 Chronicles
Lamentations	

At last the contents of the Old Testament had been brought together. What marker would you choose for the men who helped to give us the Old Testament? What would you say to honor those who taught, wrote, copied, and compiled the ancient records and so passed on to us more than half our Bible?

On the trail down which the Bible has come to us, you might like to erect a tablet with a tribute something like this one:

To Jewish people of faith,
Chosen of God,
And inspired by him
To give us,
In the Old Testament,
Records of experiences with him.

Bible passages used as source material in this chapter include the books of Ezra and Nehemiah.

8

The Old Testament in a New Language

Flavius Josephus once fought as a soldier and ruled as governor of Galilee, but it is not for his fighting or his governorship that he is best known. He is famous, even today, for his writings about the Jewish people. For he tells much of their history during the four centuries just before Jesus was born.

In one book, Josephus has included a story about how the Old Testament was translated into the Greek language.

When Alexander the Great conquered Egypt, that country began to take on the culture of Greece. Ptolemy, king of Egypt, built a great library at Alexandria. It is said to have housed the greatest collection of manuscripts the world has ever known.

When you think of a library, in your mind you see shelves and shelves and shelves of books, most of them small. The library at Alexandria was made up of more than seven hundred thousand bulky scrolls!

ΠΈΡΙΚΛΗΣ

Library at Alexandria housed almost a million bulky scrolls.

The older scrolls were written on papyrus, the newer ones on parchment. For parchment had been developed in Pergamum, a city in the country we now call Turkey. There, men had learned to dry the skins of animals and prepare them for writing. This material had been named "pergament," for the city. Later it was called "parchment."

Ptolemy, king of Egypt, boasted of this fine library at Alexandria. He was amazed one day when someone called attention to the fact that in it there was no copy of the sacred books of the Jews. There did not even exist a copy of the Jewish Scriptures in the Greek language.

Ptolemy knew that many Jews lived in Alexandria, some of them because they wanted to; others because they had been deported there. He made a plan. First he ordered the release of Jewish slaves in Alexandria.

Then he wrote a letter to the high priest in Jerusalem.

"Take this letter to Jerusalem," Ptolemy ordered. "Tell the high priest of the Temple that I have released the Jewish slaves here. Take with you gifts of gold and precious stones. When you have delivered my gifts, present the letter."

The messengers obeyed.

In Jerusalem the high priest received his visitors. He broke the royal seal and unrolled the letter. It began:

> King Ptolemy to Eleazar the high priest, sendeth greetings.

On and on the high priest read, for the king had written much about the Jews who lived in Alexandria. The letter told of many freed from slavery and given good positions. Then came the request:

> I have determined to procure an interpretation of your law and to have it translated out of Hebrew into Greek, and to be deposited in my library.
>
> Thou wilt therefore do well to choose out and send to me men of a good character, who are now elders in age, and six in number out of every tribe. These . . . must be skilful in the laws, and of abilities to make an accurate interpretation of them.

Immediately the high priest chose seventy-two wise old men who not only knew Jewish Law but were also skilled in both the Hebrew and Greek languages. These he sent to Alexandria. With them they carried gifts for the king and a copy of the Hebrew Law which the Jerusalem Jews declared accurate.

In Alexandria, the seventy-two men were received with great ceremonies. For twelve days they were feasted and entertained. Then they were led across a long bridge to an island.

Down by the sea, in a quiet house, the seventy-two men from Jerusalem began the work of translating the Jewish Law from Hebrew into the Greek language.

Long hours they worked, and in seventy-two days the five books of the Pentateuch were completed.

The delighted king ordered the scrolls stored in the great library.

He gave each of the seventy-two workers three fine garments, two talents of gold, an expensive drinking cup, and a piece of furniture from the room where they had been feasted in Alexandria. Then he sent them home.

Josephus, who wrote that story, lived several hundred years after Ptolemy was king of Egypt. He must have heard the tale as it was passed down from generation to generation just as historians today hear stories.

Yet most of the big facts he gives have been proved accurate.

What are some of these recognized facts?

The conquests of Alexander the Great in 322 B.C. did open the way for Greek culture to spread throughout the world. At least seventy Greek cities had been established, including Alexandria. Throughout the empire, Greek philosophers, scientists, architects, artists, and colonists spread their learning. Men's thinking was broadening. Great universities and libraries were established. Greek became the language of the known world.

Ptolemy did rule Egypt for a part of the third and fourth centuries, and established a great library in Alexandria.

Jewish people did live in most of the new cities of the Greek world. Alexander had given them a special invitation to settle there, and many had accepted. Some had joined the older Jewish settlements in Babylon; a large group had gone to Alexandria. An old map shows their occupancy of about half the city.

Jewish people of that time learned and spoke a form of the Greek language, especially in the new cities—"Translation Greek," some historians call it.

Historians agree that a complete translation of the Old Testament into Greek was made in the third century B.C. It appeared at Alexandria, and was called "The Septuagint," from the Greek word meaning "seventy."

This translation became the Bible of the Greek-speaking Jewish people of that day and continued as such long after the birth of Jesus.

Many of the Old Testament passages quoted in the

New Testament are taken from the Septuagint. This explains why you often cannot find in your Old Testament, the exact words that are quoted from it in the New Testament. For your Old Testament was not translated from a Greek edition.

Jesus himself was familiar with the Greek version of the Old Testament and often quoted from it. Copies of the Septuagint became a chief source for Bible students and translators.

The land of Judah, along with other countries, continued under Greek rule for many years. At one time it was annexed to Egypt, at another to Syria.

One Syrian ruler sought to impose the worship of heathen gods on his Jewish subjects. He ordered the Scriptures of the Jews burned and an altar to Jupiter set up in the very courtyard of the Temple at Jerusalem. When a heathen priest began to offer sacrifices there, the Jewish people pelted him with yellow thick-skinned citrons, but they could not prevent the burning of the sacred scrolls.

In 63 B.C. Rome completed its conquest of the world of that day. General Pompey led the siege against Jerusalem.

Its defenders barricaded themselves inside the Temple.

The attackers tore down great sections of the city wall and their battering rams hurled huge stones against the Temple.

At last Jerusalem surrendered.

Forty years later, Herod was appointed governor of Judea. Early in his reign he gave orders for clearing away what remained of the old Temple and building a new one. The structure was torn down a little at a time, and the rebuilding done in sections. In whatever section remained, the Jews continued their worship.

For more than fifty years the work of building Herod's Temple went on. And always, in the most honored spot, the Jews kept their copies of the ancient Scripture scrolls which they had treasured and carefully preserved.

These included not only the Law and the history of the Jews, but all of the other books of the Old Testament.

Devout men studied these scrolls and some of them found more than law and a record of the past. They found a hope for the future.

As they read the book of Isaiah, they sensed the truth that God would one day send a Deliverer, a Redeemer from sin.

For the inspired prophet had looked down the centuries. He had written of a King who would one day rule Israel.

The hearts of faithful Jews were gladdened when they read Isaiah's words:

> Unto us a child is born,
> Unto us a son is given:
> And the government shall be upon
>   his shoulder:
> And his name shall be called Wonderful,

Counsellor,
The mighty God,
The everlasting Father,
The Prince of Peace.

The Jewish people waited for a new day.

Do you think that Greek leaders were used of God in giving a Greek Old Testament to the world when most people knew only that language?

Do you think heathen kings helped, in ways they did not know, to preserve the worship of the Lord God?

What about the unknown scholars who learned the Greek and Hebrew languages well enough to translate the Old Testament from Hebrew into Greek? Do you think they too deserve a marker on the long trail down which the Bible has come to us?

An inscription in their honor might read:

To ancient scholars
Who respected learning
And used their skills
More than two thousand years ago,
To make the first translation of the Old Testament
Into the Greek language.

9

Before There Was a New Testament

In the Temple at Jerusalem, errand boys searched among the old scrolls stored in the library.

"King Herod is asking the chief priests and scribes a hard question," one explained. "He says Wise Men from the east are seeking directions to find a king of the Jews who has been born. They say a star guided them to this country."

"King of the Jews!" All the errand boys repeated the words. A few almost sneered at the thought.

"Herod rules us as king," one boy remarked, "but he was appointed by the Romans. Our Israelite people have not chosen a king of their own for hundreds of years!"

Most of the boys nodded in agreement.

"We Jews will have our own king some day," one boy argued. "My father says that it is promised by the old prophets."

"I've found the book," the first boy announced at last.

He lifted the scroll of Micah from its place and carried it to a scribe. The scribe unrolled the book and read it for some time. He talked with the chief priests and the other scribes.

They carried the scroll to the king and made their report. "The king of the Jews will be born in Bethlehem. The prophet Micah says so."

They read aloud from the scroll:

> And thou Bethlehem,
> In the land of Juda, . . .
> Out of thee shall come a Governor,
> That shall rule my people Israel.

King Herod frowned. He was still frowning when he returned to his visitors and directed them to Bethlehem.

On to Bethlehem the Wise Men went. There, guided by the star which they had been following, they found a young mother with her child.

"His name is Jesus," she must have told the Wise Men. "Even before he was born, an angel told me what to name him." The angel said:

> He shall be great,
> And shall be called the Son of the Highest:
> And the Lord God shall give unto him
> The throne of his father David: . . .
> Of his kingdom there shall. be no end."

The Wise Men worshiped the child and presented the rich gifts they had brought. Then they went away.

In the home which Mary and Joseph made for him, the child Jesus grew. By the time he was twelve years old, he realized that he had a very special work to do in the world. He called God "Father," and he spoke of this work as "my Father's business."

Day by day the boy learned from his teachers; year by year, he grew taller. And all the time, he was increasing "in favour with God and man."

When he was thirty years old, he declared himself on God's side. He was baptized before a crowd of people. Soon he began his special work.

One day, in the synagogue of his home town, he read to his neighbors from the scroll of Isaiah. These were the words he read.

> The Spirit of the Lord is upon me,
> Because he hath anointed me to preach the gospel
>   to the poor;
> He hath sent me to heal the brokenhearted,
> To preach deliverance to the captives,
> And recovering of sight to the blind,
> To set at liberty them that are bruised,
> To preach the acceptable year of the Lord.

Then he made a startling announcement.

"The prophet is speaking of me," Jesus said. "God has sent me to declare the good news of the gospel, to lead all kinds of people into healing fellowship with him. That is my work in the world."

Capernaum on the Sea of Galilee.

The people were amazed. They so resented his claim to be the Deliverer whom God had promised that they tried to push him over a cliff near the town.

Quietly Jesus made his way to other parts of the country. He began to make more and more friends.

In little synagogues all over Galilee he taught the gospel of the kingdom. And wherever he went, he healed sick men and women and told them about the kingdom of God.

Yet when Jesus spoke of the kingdom, he was not thinking of a throne in Judea or even in Rome. He was not thinking of a golden crown or of conquering armies that would wipe out the enemies of the Jews. He was thinking of something much bigger and more important.

Jesus was thinking of God ruling in the hearts of people and wiping out evil from their lives. He was thinking of men and women and boys and girls so full of God's love that they would always be helping one another, comforting one another, and ministering to needy people, no matter who or where they were.

His listeners found it hard to think of a kingdom of that kind. Especially did the religious leaders of the Jews resent such an idea. The hearts of these scribes and Pharisees were so full of selfishness and pride that their minds were closed to the gospel of love which Jesus preached. They hated him even more when he saw through their religious forms and pretenses to the evil in their hearts, and they resented his popularity with many of the people.

When Jesus forgave a man's sins one day, Jewish leaders accused him of being disrespectful to God. "Only God can forgive sins," they said.

Jesus must have smiled to himself.

He went on preaching and healing and helping people. And he chose special friends to help him in his work.

It was months later that he explained that he was the Son of God and that God was working through him to deliver people from the rule of evil in their hearts and bring them to fellowship with him.

Opposition to Jesus' work increased. In the Sermon on the Mount and on many other occasions, he taught people about the kingdom he had come to establish, the kingdom where the love of God rules in the heart and casts out all sin, the kingdom where this love of God in the heart flows out in helpfulness to all people.

"Only in this kind of living can people really know God," Jesus explained. "And fellowship with God is the most important thing any individual can have."

The religious leaders of the Jews were furious. They had taught the people that they could earn fellowship with God by keeping hundreds and hundreds of rules. "The law of Moses is the most important thing in the world," they argued.

"I have not come to destroy God's laws," Jesus explained. "I have come to accomplish the thing that the Law has pointed you to, to show you the way to God.

"I am the way," he declared. "No man comes to the Father but by me."

The Jewish leaders were so angry that they began to plan to destroy such a teacher.

Jesus was not surprised. He had faced the fact that establishing the rule of God's love would not be easy. He knew the hate and the dangers he would face. Yet he held fast to the steadfast purpose of his life.

"The Son of man is come to seek and to save that which was lost," he said one day, and he tried to explain that any man who is out of fellowship with God is like a sheep lost in a dangerous woods with no shepherd to take care of him.

"What is God really like?" people wondered.

"He who has seen me has seen the Father God," Jesus told them. "I and my Father are one. Have faith in me."

As he kept on preaching, Jesus did not stop healing people and helping them when they were troubled.

Yet he realized that it would take more than gracious words or even kind deeds to bring people into fellowship with God.

He hinted the cost to himself once when he said, "I came not to be ministered unto, but to minister and to give my life a ransom for many."

"I am the Good Shepherd," Jesus explained. "The Good Shepherd gives his life for the sheep."

One day Jesus told his best friends plainly that his enemies would kill him. "No man takes my life from me," he continued. "I lay it down of myself. I have power to lay it down, and I have power to take it again."

At another time he said, "The Son of man must be delivered into the hands of sinful men, and be crucified, and the third day rise again."

One day Jewish leaders had Jesus arrested. He was falsely charged with disloyalty to the Roman Government and with seeking to destroy the Jewish religion. His accusers sought a sentence of death by crucifixion.

"I find no fault in this man," the Roman judge declared.

Yet, to please Jewish politicians, he gave the sentence. On a hill called Calvary, Jesus died.

His body was buried and the tomb sealed.

Three days later amazing news spread throughout Jerusalem,

"The Lord is risen!"

Still, religious leaders would not accept Jesus as the Christ. The King of the Jews had come, and they had not recognized him. "He came unto his own, and his own received him not."

For almost six weeks, the risen Christ walked among his friends in Jerusalem. He comforted them and helped them understand what had happened.

One day he called them together and gave them special work to do.

"Go to people all over the world," Jesus told his followers. "Preach the gospel which I have taught and lived among you. Tell people to trust the God I have shown to you. Teach them to live by making his love rule in their hearts.

"I will be with you as you work. My Holy Spirit in your hearts and minds will guide you as you share my gospel and live by my love. Just as God sent me into the world, so I am sending you."

On the trail down which our Bible has come to us, we have, in this chapter, stopped to look at about thirty-three years, years *before there was a New Testament*. We have focused on the coming of Jesus Christ and the beginning of the Christian religion.

In previous chapters of this book, the letters "B.C."

were used with dates, the letters meaning "Before Christ."

In the remainder of this book, dates will be A.D., for our way of counting years begins with the birth of Jesus Christ. And you recognize A.D. as the abbreviation of the Latin words, *anno Domini,* which mean "in the year of our Lord." Dates today tell the number of years that have passed since Jesus was born.

The first four books of the New Testament tell of Jesus' life when he lived on earth. What Jesus' friends did and said and continued to do and say after he went back to his Father is told in the other twenty-three books.

> Before the New Testament,
> There was Jesus Christ,
> And there were people
> Who needed him.
> "The Father sent the Son
> To be the Saviour of the world."
>
> The New Testament tells of Jesus Christ
> And his gospel.
> And in the New Testament,
> God is showing himself
> To you and to me
> And to all people everywhere.

Bible passages used as source material in this chapter include the four Gospels, especially Matthew 2.

10

Letter Writers

In the city of Corinth, Greece, a man sat at a loom weaving. Skilfully, he passed the shuttle of goat's-hair yarn through the warp threads on the loom. Carefully, with a heavy beam, he pounded each new thread firmly into the web of cloth that slowly grew longer with each stroke of the beam.

The sound of the loom echoed through the room, and Priscilla looked up from her sewing and spoke.

"You have been weaving on that tent ever since you came from the synagogue this morning," she said. "Where did you learn to weave, Paul?"

"In Tarsus," Paul answered. "Before I went to the school of the rabbis in Jerusalem, I was trained to weave tents."

Priscilla nodded. "I remember now," she said. "You smiled when you learned that Aquila and I were tent-makers. We have been so glad to have you help us in our work."

"I have been glad to find work to do," Paul declared. "This way I can weave tents and support myself as I preach the gospel of Jesus Christ."

"You were a Jewish teacher in Jerusalem, weren't you?" Priscilla asked.

"Yes," Paul replied. "I was a Pharisee, a member of the Sanhedrin court of the Jews.

"In Jerusalem I stood by and watched Christians being stoned to death. I myself hunted down the followers of the Lord Jesus and arrested them and had them put into prison.

"I even got letters authorizing me to hunt down Christians in other cities. And then—"

Paul waited a moment.

"And then one day I knew the Lord Jesus was speaking to me. The Christians had told the truth. Their Lord had indeed risen from the dead. He was calling me to follow him and to preach his gospel. That is why I came to Corinth."

"You have spoken in the synagogue every day," Priscilla reminded Paul. "Don't work too hard, Paul."

Paul smiled. "There is so much to be done," he told Priscilla. "You and your husband have been kind to me, and I want to do my part in helping you make tents. Yet now I will rest my arms for a while. The heavy beam of the loom tires them."

Paul rose from the loom, but he did not lie down or sit idly in the doorway.

Instead he got out papyrus, pen, and ink, and called Timothy to come to him.

"The new Christians back in Thessalonica need instruction and encouragement," Paul told Timothy. "Let's write them a letter."

He began to speak, and as he spoke, Timothy wrote the words in the Greek language.

"Paul, and Silvanus, and Timotheus," the letter began, giving the names of the writers first as letters did in the first century A.D.

"Unto the church of the Thessalonians," it continued. "Grace be unto you, and peace, from God our Father, and the Lord Jesus Christ."

"We thank God for you," the letter went on. "We pray for you. And we remember your faith in Jesus Christ, your love for him, and the work you are doing because of that love."

The letter went on to tell the Christians in Thessalonica more about Jesus Christ and how he wants his followers to live. A part of it said:

> Rejoice evermore.
> Pray without ceasing.
> In everything give thanks:
> For this is the will of God in Christ Jesus
>   concerning you.

Paul asked the Christians in Thessalonica to pray for him, and to read the letter aloud to all the Christians in the city. He closed with a benediction: "The grace of our Lord Jesus Christ be with you."

Timothy put the sheets together and rolled them into a scroll which he sent to Thessalonica.

Today, in your Bible, you can find First Thessalonians, a translation of a copy of that letter of Paul's. Scholars tell us that, of all Paul's letters which have been preserved in our Bible, First Thessalonians was probably the first to be written. Fragments of a copy of this epistle have been found which date back to about A.D. 200.

Paul himself had no idea that his letter would be preserved as a book. Yet, inspired by the Holy Spirit, he so wrote that his first "epistle to the Thessalonians" has come to us as one of the thirteen books credited to him in our New Testament.

If you will look in your Bible at each of those thirteen books, you will find them addressed to Christians or "saints" in various places. You will also notice that they begin much alike. Each one mentions the name of the writer and the name of the person or persons to whom the letter is addressed. It goes on to speak of Jesus Christ and to tell something of what it means to trust him and live as a Christian.

Some of the letters of Paul are more personal than the one to the Christians in Thessalonica.

Paul wrote one of these letters to his friend Philemon.

For many years Paul had been a missionary. Many times he had been imprisoned for preaching the gospel.

Some New Testament books were written from a Roman prison.

About the year A.D. 62 he was arrested again and thrown into a dungeon in Rome.

In the dim light that filtered through a high, small opening in the wall, Paul could see the stones in the floor of the cell. They reminded him of the Appian Way that led outside the city. It was paved with the same kind of stones. Paul knew that many of his Christian friends were being led down that road to their death.

He moved restlessly, and the chain on his wrist clanked. The soldier to whom he was bound stirred, too. Then both went back to sleep.

One day Paul had a visitor.

"Do you remember me?" the visitor asked.

Paul leaned closer to peer into his visitor's face. He smiled.

"Of course," he replied. "You are my friend Onesimus, now a follower of my Lord. You are a Christian."

Onesimus nodded.

"I am a runaway slave," he told Paul. "In Colossae I took money from my master Philemon. Now that I am a Christian I am sorry. What must I do about it?"

"You must decide that," Paul said. "You know that a Christian must be honest."

"Do you realize what my master can do to me if I return to Colossae?" Onesimus asked.

Paul nodded his head. He knew that the law allowed a slave owner to have an escaped slave beaten, branded, or even put to death.

"I know," he told Onesimus. "Yet Philemon is a Christian."

"Do you think that will make a difference?" Onesimus asked.

"I do not know," Paul answered. "Come back to me when you have reached your decision."

He watched as Onesimus turned away and walked out through the shadows.

The Roman soldier spoke. "You expect a great deal of a Christian," he said.

"Yes," Paul agreed, "but our Lord can give great courage to a Christian. He can make a man brave in spite of his fears."

"Do you think the young slave will return?" the soldier asked.

"I think so," Paul said. "I must write Philemon a letter."

The soldier moved writing materials closer, and Paul bent down to see the page as he began to write.

Paul, a prisoner of Jesus Christ, and Timothy our brother, unto Philemon our dearly beloved, and fellow labourer.

"Timothy will appreciate being included," Paul said to himself. "He, too, knows Philemon."

He continued his letter.

I thank God for you, and I do not forget to pray for you. I am writing this letter to ask a favor of you.

Paul told about Onesimus, whom he had led to become a Christian, and who had been kind to him in the prison. Then he asked the favor.

I know Onesimus is your servant, but he is also our Christian brother. I myself will pay whatever Onesimus owes you, and I hope you will receive him just as you would receive me.

Paul added greetings from other Christian friends in Rome and closed the letter with a prayer of benediction: "The grace of our Lord Jesus Christ be with your spirit."

If you will turn through your New Testament, you can read all of the very short letter which Paul wrote to Philemon.

And in a letter Paul later wrote to the church at Colossae, he mentioned Onesimus as a "beloved brother" in that group of Christians.

In your New Testament, you will also find letters written by Peter, by Jude, and by James, who was a pastor.

Peter's letter mentions the fact that he and other New Testament writers were careful to write accurately. It says:

We have not followed cunningly devised fables,
When we made known unto you the power
And coming of our Lord Jesus Christ,
But were eyewitnesses of his majesty.

One letter, the epistle to the Hebrews, does not name the writer.

The very last book in the Bible is a letter directed to seven churches in Asia. One church must have passed it on to another. That letter tells where the writer had been exiled for preaching the gospel and how he came to write the letter.

> John to the seven churches which are in Asia:
> I . . . was in the isle that is called Patmos,
> For the word of God,
> And for the testimony of Jesus Christ.
> I was in the Spirit on the Lord's day,
> And heard behind me a great voice, as of
>   a trumpet,
> Saying, . . . What thou seest, write in a book,
> And send it unto the seven churches.

Each one of these New Testament letters was written to meet a need, and different people in different places had varying needs. Each writer had his own individual personality. So their letters are not alike.

Yet, in one way, all these letters are alike. They are alike in purpose. For they were written to help people to know Jesus Christ and his gospel.

While the writers had no idea that the contents of their letters would be preserved as books, the Holy Spirit so directed their thinking that what they wrote has become a part of the New Testament section of our Bible and continues to guide Christians today.

Of the twenty-seven books in the New Testament, twenty-two are called epistles, or letters.

How would you like to honor Paul and John and the other busy men who took time to respond to the inspiration of God's Spirit and to write these twenty-two books?

What inscription would you choose for another marker on the trail down which the Bible has come to us? Would it be something like this one?

To the apostle Paul
And other Christian men
Whom God inspired
To write letters
And so to share the gospel
Of the Lord Jesus.

Bible passages used as source materials in this chapter include the book of Acts, especially chapter 18; and selections from the epistles of Paul, Peter, and John.

11

Biographers and Historians

John Mark looked at his old friend and sighed. "Peter is growing feeble," he thought. "It has been thirty years since he saw Jesus Christ leave this earth. He can't live a great deal longer. Who will tell us about Jesus when Peter and Jesus' other intimate friends are gone?"

Aloud, Mark said, "I have always loved to hear you tell about your days with Jesus. Why don't you write down the things you have told me? Christians need to know these things, and some day there will be no one living who really knew Jesus when he was here on earth."

Peter shook his head. "I am too old to do a job like that," he answered. "And besides, I must go on preaching. Why don't you make a record of the life of our Lord? I will be glad to tell you all I know about him, and so will other people."

Could he write a book about Jesus? Mark began to wonder about it. To whom would he talk besides Peter?

What questions would he ask? Would he be able to find memoranda of some of the things Jesus had said? Would some of Jesus' friends have jotted down notes? Both Jewish and Roman court records might help a bit.

All of these questions may have passed through John Mark's mind. He asked some of them. He talked again with people, especially with Peter. Here and there he found a few bits of papyrus with helpful writing on them. He made his own notes, and he made a decision.

One day he stacked sheets of papyrus high on his table and got out ink and a fresh pen.

"I hope I can remember all that Peter and the others have told me," Mark mused aloud. He sat quietly for a few moments. Then, in the Greek language, he began to write: "The beginning of the gospel of Jesus Christ, the Son of God."

"Peter remembers more about Jesus than anyone," Mark thought to himself as he worked on at the task he had chosen. And because Mark was a follower of the Lord Jesus, he thanked God for Peter's good memory and prayed that he himself might do good work.

Mark reminded his readers of Isaiah's prophecy that a messenger would prepare the way for the Messiah's coming. Then he told about John the Baptist who had preached to the people and had baptized Jesus.

Mark wrote down God's words of approval when he said of Jesus, "Thou art my beloved Son, in whom I am well pleased."

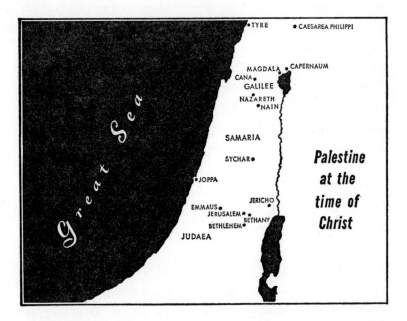

On and on Mark wrote. Carefully he chose his words and formed each letter. He thought of Greek readers especially, and explained some of the Jewish customs that they might not understand. Occasionally he used an Aramaic word which Peter himself had used in telling about Jesus.

Mark wrote mostly about deeds Jesus had done—his miracles. Other Gospels tell of these same miracles, but Mark alone mentions the name of blind Bartimaeus. Mark alone tells of the green grass on the hillside where Jesus fed five thousand men in addition to the women and children.

For days and days and weeks Mark wrote. At last his manuscript was finished. The pages were put together and rolled into a scroll.

If you will open your Bible to the second book in the New Testament, you can read a translation of the book Mark wrote. But it is not the second biography of Jesus that was written; it is the first! "The Gospel According to Mark" is the first biography of Jesus to be preserved in our Bible.

Matthew's Gospel was the second to be written. His book tells of many of the same events as Mark's, but it is longer. For Matthew tells many more things which Jesus said as well as did.

Matthew wrote of the name "Emmanuel" which was to be given to Jesus. He told of the visit of the Wise Men and of Mary and Joseph carrying the Child to safety in Egypt.

Matthew had been a tax collector. He was accustomed to keeping records. His position demanded accurate ones.

Jesus had known of Matthew's ability when he called him to be his special follower. He also knew what a man can do when he dedicates his ability to God.

Do you think Matthew had jotted down, on bits of papyrus or parchment, the words his Gospel gives us from Jesus' famous Sermon on the Mount and other teachings? Do you suppose Matthew kept a diary of some of the things Jesus did as he and his disciples went about the country? Was it Matthew's habit of carefulness that gave us the genealogy of Jesus in the first chapter of the Gospel of Matthew?

Another biographer of Jesus was a physician. How a busy doctor found time to write a book, nobody knows; but even today, doctors sometimes do that. Luke was not a Jew, as Mark and Matthew were. He was a Gentile, but he had traveled with Paul and understood Jewish customs. He had studied medicine, perhaps in the famous school at Tarsus.

Luke begins his gospel by stating his purpose:

Forasmuch as many have taken in hand to set forth
    in order
A declaration of those things which are most surely
    believed among us,
Even as they delivered them unto us,
Which from the beginning were eyewitnesses,
And ministers of the word;
It seemed good to me also,
Having had perfect understanding of all things
From the very first,
To write unto thee in order, most excellent
    Theophilus,
That thou mightest know the certainty
Of those things, wherein thou hast been instructed.

Luke must have done a great deal of research. He must have read the letters and Gospels which had already been written, and consulted with people who had known Jesus.

Only Luke tells of the healing of the woman whose

back had been crooked for eighteen years. Only in his Gospel do we find the parables of the good Samaritan and of the prodigal son.

Only Luke tells the story of Zacchaeus, and of Jesus meeting two of his disciples on the road to Emmaus.

Because he was a physician, Luke was especially interested in occasions when Jesus healed people. He was careful to tell about each one.

Luke's Gospel is the only one which records the angel's visit to Mary before the birth of Jesus. It also tells our best-loved Christmas story of the angels' song to the shepherds and of their visit to Bethlehem.

Do you suppose Luke heard these stories from Mary, the mother of Jesus? He made a record of all of them in "The Gospel According to Luke." When it was completed and the sheets of parchment put together, they made a scroll almost thirty feet long.

This busy doctor also wrote another book telling some of the adventures of the followers of Jesus after Jesus went away.

It is in this second book by Luke that we read that believers in Jesus were called Christians first at Antioch. Luke's second book tells of the coming of the Holy Spirit and how that same Spirit guided these Christians in their speaking and in their work. This book—the book of Acts—tells of new churches being formed, of the persecutions of Christians, and of Paul's great missionary journeys.

Luke had been with Paul during many of his travels, and his record is vivid. Some modern writers say his description of Paul's shipwreck is the best available picture of sea travel of the first century.

The fourth Gospel in the New Testament is a biography of Jesus credited to a man named John. Many scholars think this is John the son of Zebedee. Certainly, the writer had intimate knowledge of Jesus and his teachings.

John is quite clear as to the purpose of his book. Speaking of it, he says:

> Many other signs truly did Jesus
> In the presence of his disciples,
> Which are not written in this book:
> But these are written,
> That ye might believe that Jesus is the
>   Christ, the Son of God;
> And that believing ye might have life
> Through his name.

The writer of John's Gospel uses the word "life" a great deal. He is speaking of spiritual life, the kind of life and spiritual energy that are rooted in trust in and reliance on the Lord Jesus. He quotes many of Jesus' promises and gives us the "little gospel" which you know as John 3:16.

John tells much of how Jesus thought and felt about his Father.

Adding much to the records made by Mark, Matthew, and Luke, and enriching some of the events they also

report, John tells of the raising of Lazarus from the dead
and of the breakfast which seven of Jesus' disciples had
with him after his resurrection. It is John who gives Jesus'
words beginning, "Let not your heart be troubled."

John's Gospel reveals a writer with a good memory and
a talent for explaining truth. Jesus had promised his
disciples such help. One day, as he finished talking with
them, he had said:

> The Comforter, which is the Holy Ghost,
> Whom the Father will send in my name,
> He shall teach you all things,
> And bring all things to your remembrance,
> Whatsoever I have said unto you.
> Peace I leave with you.

So John, along with the other three writers of the
Gospels, used a memory sharpened by the Holy Spirit. Yet
John realized that his record was not complete. He says:

> There are also many other things
> Which Jesus did,
> The which, if they should be written
>   every one,
> I suppose that even the world itself
> Could not contain the books
> That should be written.

Probably neither Matthew nor Mark, neither Luke nor
John, was satisfied with his manuscript about Jesus, for
words cannot tell the wonder of the Lord Jesus Christ.

Yet, moved by the Holy Spirit, they made the Gospel record. And along with other devout writers of the New Testament, they produced books which still guide men and women to the truth of God as revealed in his Son.

Like the messages of the Old Testament, the writings which make up our New Testament are profitable "for doctrine, for reproof, for correction, for instruction in righteousness." All twenty-seven books were written that men might believe on the Lord Jesus and that Christians might grow into completeness, each one thoroughly equipped for "all good works."

You will want to think of these New Testament biographers and historians as you choose markers for the trail down which the Bible has come to us. Would the inscription on their tablet read something like this one?

This tablet is dedicated
To men who believed
On the Lord Jesus Christ
With all their hearts
And wrote letters and books
To share their faith.

Bible passages used as source materials in this chapter include the four Gospels and the book of Acts.

12

Books in Hiding

"Rome is on fire!" The news spread through the city, and so did the flames. Most of the city was burned.

It was the year A.D. 64 and Nero was emperor of the Roman world. He must lay the blame on someone, and he chose the Christians. They were not an influential group, and they could make little trouble for him. Most of them were peace-loving people. They also refused to worship the Emperor as the government demanded. So the order went out.

"Seize the Christians!"

Believers in Jesus Christ were arrested and thrown into prison. Sometimes they were given a chance to save their lives.

"Worship the Emperor and you will be set free," they were told. A few did so, but most chose torture and death, rather than break loyalty to their Lord. Some were soaked in oil and burned to death; others were beheaded with swords; still others were thrown to the lions in the arena.

"Paul has been arrested!" As the Christians in Rome whispered the words to one another, they shuddered for the old missionary.

In the cold, dark dungeon where he was chained, Paul shivered and wished for the warm coat he had left in Troas. He wanted his books, and especially the parchments on which he had made notes of some of the things he wanted to tell new Christians in many places.

Some of these new Christians were not Jews, Paul knew. For Christianity had become a religion, not of Jewish people alone, but of men and women of many nationalities and many races. There were Christians in Greece, in Africa, and in many other places, as well as in Rome.

In his mind, Paul could see these Christians meeting together for worship. He knew that they read the Old Testament Scriptures. Sometimes they read letters which he and Luke and other Christian leaders had written to explain the gospel. For copies of Christian letters and scrolls had begun to be made and passed around among many churches.

As Paul thought of these new churches, he almost forgot how cold it was in his dungeon. In his letter to his friend Timothy, he did not mention the coat until almost the end.

Instead, he told Timothy that God could make him brave and help him to love people, even in time of danger.

"I am not ashamed to be a follower of the Lord Jesus," Paul wrote. "I know whom I have believed, and am persuaded that he is able to keep that which I have committed unto him."

"Keep on studying and preaching," Paul cautioned his young preacher friend. "Live as the Lord Jesus taught, and remember that the Scriptures of the Old Testament can help you, for God speaks through them."

"I am now ready to be offered," Paul continued. "The time of my death is near at hand. I have kept faith with my Lord, and I know that he will take care of me in the way that is best, even in death and afterwards."

As usual, Paul closed his letter with a prayer: "The Lord Jesus Christ be with thy spirit. Grace be with you."

In spite of persecution, the preaching of the gospel continued. Churches increased! And Christian scribes continued to make copies of the gospels and of Christian letters.

The form of these manuscripts was changing. No longer were the sheets of papyrus put together in rolls. Instead, pages of vellum or parchment were folded together one by one, or in groups of two, three, or four sheets each. These were then sewed together as leaves in a book. The volume so made was called a codex. The four Gospels were sometimes fastened together in one volume, and Paul's letters in another.

Persecution of the Christians continued for more than two hundred years, with only brief periods of tolerance.

At least nine Roman emperors launched fierce attacks on the Christian religion.

By this time, many of the old scrolls had worn out. Others had been lost or destroyed. But copies in the new codex form had been preserved. Other books about Jesus and his gospel had appeared.

In 303 the Emperor Diocletian launched the most systematic, widespread, and determined persecution which Christians had yet faced.

"Stamp out Christianity," he ordered. "The followers of Jesus are troublesome. They will not worship the Emperor as good Romans do. Put them to death. Destroy their buildings. Burn the Christian books! Stop those Christians!"

Individual Christians and church groups heard the order. They sorted their books and decided which ones were worth risking their lives to keep. They chose those which best represented the life of the Lord Jesus and the Christian faith. These they hid in caves and rocks, in ruined church buildings, and in other strange places. And, in secret, men made more copies of these Christian books.

Most of the Christians remained loyal to their religion.

In the court of Diocletian, young Constantine watched many die rather than surrender their books or their faith in the Lord Jesus.

What kind of religion could make a man brave like that? Who was this Jesus the Christians talked about?

Had he actually risen from the dead as they claimed? These thoughts haunted the young man.

When he became emperor some years later, Constantine still wondered about those men and women who had been so fearless even in the face of death. In 313 he ordered freedom of worship and made Christianity a part of the official religion of the Roman Empire.

Constantine was also interested in the books which the Christians valued so highly. He sought out those hidden treasures and ordered fifty copies made by hand for the churches of Constantinople.

Worn manuscripts were brought from their hiding places. Christians began to collect the books which told about their religion. Some, they decided, deserved to be read in their churches each Sunday, along with passages from the Old Testament.

The books chosen differed in Egypt, in Syria, and in Rome, but Christians of all countries included the four Gospels and the letters of Paul. Later others were added.

By the year 393, there emerged a list of twenty-seven books that had proved themselves to Christians during the years. They were the same twenty-seven books that make up our New Testament today. Together with the thirty-nine books of the Old Testament, these books began to be called the Bible of Christians.

They were, of course, written by hand, in capital letters. These letters were large and rounded, with no space between either sentences or words, but sometimes certain words were abbreviated and a mark made over them to indicate that they were sacred. If those old manuscripts had been written in English rather than Greek, the first four verses of John's Gospel might have looked something like this passage:

INTHEBEGINNINGWASTHEWORDANDTHEWORD
WASWITHGODANDTHEWORDWASGODTHESAME
WASINTHEBEGINNINGWITHGODALLTHINGS
WEREMADEBYHIMANDWITHOUTHIMWASNOT
ANYTHINGMADETHATWASMADEINHIMWAS
LIFEANDTHELIFEWASTHELIGHTOFMEN

Manuscripts continued to be written in this way until the ninth century.

One of the oldest and most famous of the old Greek manuscripts, the Codex Sinaiticus, was discovered more than a thousand years later by a German professor named Tischendorf.

Visiting the library of the Convent of St. Catherine, at the foot of Mount Sinai one day, he found a large basket full of old parchments.

He looked closer and was amazed to see a number of pages of a very old Greek manuscript which he recognized as part of the Bible. He was told by the librarian that other pages had been burned.

Tischendorf's excitement made the monks so suspicious that they would not allow him to see all the contents of the basket. He was, however, permitted to take forty-three sheets with him to examine.

When he returned, suspicion had grown, and he was denied permission to see more of the manuscripts. Later, he appealed to the Russian Government for help in systematic research in the East.

As a result, Tischendorf returned to the monastery almost fifteen years after his first visit. This is a part of his report of that later visit:

"I was taking a walk with the steward of the convent in the neighborhood, and as we returned, towards sunset, he begged me to take some refreshment with him in his cell.

"Scarcely had we entered the room, when resuming our former subject of conversation, he said, 'And I, too, have read a Septuagint.' . . .

"So saying he took down from the corner of the room a bulky kind of volume, wrapped in a red cloth, and laid it before me. I unrolled the cover and discovered to my great surprise, not only those fragments which fifteen years before I had taken out of the basket, but other parts of the Old Testament, the New Testament complete, and in addition, the Epistle of Barnabas and a part of the Pastor of Hermas.

"Full of joy which this time I had the self-command to conceal from the steward and the rest of the community, I asked, as if in a careless way, for permission to take the manuscript into my sleeping chamber to look over it more at leisure. There by myself I could give way to the transport of joy which I felt. I knew that I held in my hand the most precious biblical treasure in existence."

This Greek codex was carried to Russia, where it was copied and then photographed.

It remained in Leningrad (formerly St. Petersburg) until 1933, when it was sold to the British Museum in London for more than half a million dollars.

The manuscript is written on antelope skins, and has more than three hundred pages, each thirteen and a half by fifteen inches. Each page has four columns, except in the poetical books, where each page has only two columns. The words are handwritten, in capital letters, with twelve to fourteen letters to a line. It is not dated, but students of ancient manuscripts are certain that it was produced during the reign of Constantine.

Fragments of other Greek manuscripts have been found which are a hundred years older.

There have also been discovered some fragments of Latin manuscripts which are older than the Codex Sinaiticus. For Latin was the official language of the Roman Empire. While it was never in common use throughout the Roman provinces or generally used by the uneducated people of the empire, it did become the official language of Rome and of public institutions there. Latin translations of both the Old and New Testaments appeared.

Near the end of the fourth century, Jerome, a Christian

scholar, produced a Latin Bible called the Vulgate. This has been revised many times and is still the Bible of the Catholic Church. It contains not only the sixty-six books of our Bible, but others called the Apocrypha. It was not until 1228 that an edition was made with divisions into chapters. In 1555 the first Latin Bible to contain verse divisions was published.

Thousands of copies of this Latin translation were made, and these have greatly influenced later revisions and translations of the Bible into various languages, including English.

Some Bible translations were also made from the Greek language. Such editions appeared in Syria, in Ethiopia, in Arabia, in Armenia, and in a few other places.

Then came a period of history called the Dark Ages. Historians do not agree on the exact dates, but many use the year 450 to about 1150.

During this time, religious history tells us only of the work of the Roman Catholic Church. Cathedrals were built, and some missionaries sent to other countries.

In the monasteries, old copies of the Scriptures were stored, and there many manuscripts were preserved, both Latin and Greek.

Some monasteries included a special room called the *scriptorium*. There, eight or ten monks often met to copy books of many kinds. One monk would read aloud slowly from an old manuscript. The other monks would carefully print, on dried skins, the words of the reader.

One abbot gave special instruction for the copying of religious books.

Here let the scribes sit who copy out the words of the Divine Law, and likewise the hallowed sayings of Holy Fathers.

Let them beware of interspersing their own frivolities in the words they copy, nor let a trifler's hand make mistakes through haste. . . .

Let them distinguish the proper sense by colons and commas, and set the points, each one in its place. . . .

Writing books is better than planting vines, for he who plants a vine serves his belly, but he who writes a book serves his soul.

Bible books were copied in rooms called scriptoriums.

Some copies of the Scriptures were decorated in color, sometimes by nuns as well as monks. This was called "illuminating" a manuscript.

Yet, during the Dark Ages, manuscripts were not safe, even in monasteries. For these were often raided in war and many of their libraries destroyed. Books that remained were often neglected.

In the few Bible documents that remained, God was still speaking. Those who could read Greek and Latin often caught at least a part of his message. Because many people—even many priests—could not read these languages, Bible study was possible only to the few men and women who were highly educated.

Yet God continued to speak through the Scriptures and to reach out to people.

Of all these men and women who helped to spread the gospel and to preserve the Bible for us, which ones would you choose to honor with a new tablet on the trail down which the Bible has come to us?

Would you think especially of people who gave their lives rather than deny their faith? Would you remember long-ago Christians who carefully made copies of their Bible and hid them from its enemies? Would you choose wise scholars who collected old manuscripts and carefully compared them, to find those which best represented the Christian faith? Would you think especially of monastery librarians and others who copied those ancient books and kept them safe?

Perhaps for the new marker on the Bible trail, you would like to choose an inscription something like this one:

> *This tablet is dedicated*
> *To the memory of brave men,*
> *Loyal to their Lord,*
> *Who collected ancient manuscripts*
> *And preserved the Bible of Christians*
> *In spite of dungeon, fire, and sword.*

13

The First New Testament in English

The young English herdsman had slipped away from his friends, for he was timid and could not make up poems and sing them as they did. As he hid in the stable, he could still hear their taunts, "Sing, Caedmon, sing."

He heard the words even in his dreams that night. And in his dream he asked, "What shall I sing?"

The answer came, "Sing of how all things were first made."

And Caedmon sang. When he awoke, he remembered the words he had sung. One day he sang them aloud to his companions in the stables of the monastery. And he added other verses to the song.

The monks heard Caedmon's songs and declared he had received a special gift from God. They invited him to join their order and learn more about the Bible.

Caedmon did so.

He is famous in the history of the Bible as the first man

who tried to put Bible stories into the Anglo-Saxon language.

Christianity had come to Great Britain hundreds of years before the middle seventh century, when Caedmon lived. With it, monks had brought Latin Bibles to the monasteries. They made copies of them.

But Latin was a strange language, even to many of the priests and monks. Most people learned what they knew of the gospel from songs and poems which told Bible stories. People found it easy to remember these poems and to sing them. Many of them were put into writing. Such collections became known as a sort of people's Bible.

More than a hundred years later, another monk named Aldhelm also used music to preach the gospel in England. Noticing that his sermons attracted few people, Aldhelm dressed himself as a minstrel one day, and carried his harp to a bridge. As the people passed by, he played his harp. When a crowd had collected, he sang songs which put parts of the Bible into everyday words. The people listened, and later Aldhelm translated the book of Psalms into Anglo-Saxon, the language of that day.

Bede, an outstanding scholar in the monastery at Jarrow, also translated the Psalms and some of the Gospels. He worked carefully, for, he said, "I do not want my boys to read a lie, or to work to no purpose after I am gone." These translations were made especially for teaching young monks who knew no Latin.

In the ninth century, England had a king who was interested in religion. King Alfred was so convinced of the Bible's value that he ordered the Ten Commandments translated and placed at the beginning of the laws of his country.

Far in advance of most of the thinking of his day, he expressed the wish that all the freeborn youth of his kingdom "should employ themselves on nothing till they read the Scriptures!"

The English Bible of that time showed the beginning of the Lord's Prayer in these words:

> *Uren Fader dhic art in heofnas*
> *Sic gehalyed dhin noma.*

Less than a hundred years later, a young priest prepared and wrote, between the lines of a Latin Bible, an Anglo-Saxon translation of each line. Several such copies are still in existence. These translations bear little resemblance to the English language we know. The last part of the third verse of Matthew 13 read, *"Sothlice ut eode se sawere his saed to sawenne."* To the people who then lived in England, the words meant, "Behold, a sower went forth to sow."

Only a few copies of such translations were made, and to the English people as a whole, the Bible was still an unknown book.

In the year 1066 England was conquered by the Normans, and again there was a change in the language of the people; it became mixed with the French. Again a few rhyming translations appeared, and later some of the books of the Bible were translated, but only for the use of monks and nuns. For three hundred years, few attempts were made at Bible translation. Then bits of the Scriptures began to appear in the English language. Both the government and the Catholic Church frowned upon such translations.

"English is not a fit instrument for the Bible or for prayer," they declared.

A law was made that all persons reading the Scriptures in English should "forfeit land, cattle, life and goods," not only for themselves, but "for their heirs forever."

Such were conditions in 1320 when John Wycliffe was born in England. As a man, he became a priest of the Catholic Church, well educated in the Latin Bible.

Young Wycliffe was deeply concerned for people, all sorts of people. He organized bands of young priests who went about the country preaching without pay, ministering especially to the poor. Sometimes they repeated Bible passages to these people; sometimes they sang gospel stories.

Many English peasants heard the gospel for the first time from these wandering preachers, who were nicknamed Lollards. So widespread was their work that one opponent said of it, "You cannot travel anywhere in England but of every two men you meet, one will be a Lollard."

These traveling Lollards have their place in the history of the Bible, for they created and nourished a hunger for its teaching.

In his own parish, John Wycliffe began to realize that many men, both rich and poor, could not understand sermons preached in Latin. He began to preach in the English language.

He also came to a realization that the people needed a Bible in the English language.

"God's will is plainly revealed in the two Testaments," he explained, "which a Christian, well understanding, may thence gain sufficient knowledge during his pilgrimage here on earth."

Sufficient knowledge in the Bible! The Bible for the people! Such ideas were revolutionary in that day.

John Wycliffe did not stop with talk. He prepared to make an English translation of the Bible.

First, he must get together his materials for writing. His New Testament alone would need parchment from the skins of fifty or more sheep. These must be soaked in limewater to loosen the hair, then scraped clean of hair and flesh, and carefully stretched on board frames to dry. When they were dry, they must be scraped again with sharp knives to secure an even thickness, and then be rubbed smooth with pumice and chalk. This completed parchment—sometimes called vellum—must be cut into pages suitable for writing. Ink and pens must be prepared.

At last the materials were ready, and John Wycliffe and his colleagues began to translate the Latin Vulgate into the English language. They must decide what the Latin words said, and choose English words which carried the same idea.

Spelling presented difficulties, for there were no dictionaries. John Wycliffe's own last name has been found spelled in fifty different ways!

The Wycliffe translation of the New Testament was completed in 1380. Copies of it were made even as he began on an Old Testament translation. Two years later, the entire Bible appeared in the English language.

Wealthy men paid as much as two hundred dollars for a copy.

Poor peasants put their pennies together and bought parts of it.

One farmer gladly gave a load of hay and read in his own language the prayer that began:

> *Our Fadie that are in heuen,*
> *Halewid be thi name.*

Another man brought an ox and traded it for one page of a letter that Paul wrote.

Men watched in amazement as rich and poor sought to read the Word of God. One said,

"The unlearned cry after the Holy Writ, to know it, with great cost and peril of their lives."

In spite of the fact that much of Wycliffe's translation

was later declared inaccurate, his New Testament did mark the beginning of the Bible in the English language.

Yet John Wycliffe's written translation of the Bible into the English language was not his major contribution to the history of the Bible.

John Wycliffe's life was a translation of the Bible that was different and amazingly vital. His concern for all sorts of people reflected that of his Lord. He believed that the Bible should govern everyday living and sought to make it rule his own. He also believed that the Bible, and not man-made rules, should govern the church. He dared say so.

Many people caught a bit of his enthusiasm for the Bible and wanted to know more about the Book by which he lived.

More than sixty years after Wycliffe's death, exciting news from Germany reached England. A young printer named Johann Gutenberg had discovered how to use movable type in the printing of books! Centuries before that time, the art of printing had developed in China, but the process was both crude and expensive. Usually the entire page of a book was carved out, coated with ink, and pressed on paper.

Gutenberg's process, which seems so simple to us today, was completely new. It used separate letters which could be assembled into words and used over and over again. There must be suitable ink and paper, and the right kind of press. Yet Gutenberg succeeded.

The Gutenberg press.

The first complete book, using his movable type, was a Latin Bible, printed in 1455. One copy of that Gutenberg Bible is now owned by the Library of Congress in Washington, D.C., bought by the United States at a cost of more than two hundred and fifty thousand dollars.

Sixty years after Gutenberg's invention, England heard news that was still more exciting.

A young priest named Martin Luther had dared defy the pope and say that salvation comes only through the grace of God and that every individual could approach God for himself, without a priest or anyone else as a go-between.

Martin Luther was a professor in the University of Wittenberg. From a study of the Greek New Testament, he had decided that Jesus had not said, "Do penance," as the Latin Vulgate translated his words. Rather, Jesus had said, "Repent."

The young priest sought to stop the sale of indulgences by the Catholic Church, for, he said, "every Christian who feels true repentance has as of right full remission of penalty and guilt, even without letters of pardon [indulgences]."

Luther also began a translation of the Bible into the German language, basing his New Testament translation on Greek manuscripts.

To find words that everyday German people could understand, Luther spent much time questioning laborers, and even "children and mothers," to secure familiar expressions. His German New Testament was completed in 1522.

Luther also began a campaign for widespread education. He insisted that "every human being, by the time he has reached his tenth year, should be familiar with the Holy Gospels, in which the very core and marrow of his life is bound." To accomplish this end, he urged parents to send their children to school so that they might learn to read the Bible.

Luther was put out of the Catholic Church, but he continued to preach salvation by grace and to urge people to study the Scriptures.

Erasmus, of Rotterdam, made a similar emphasis on Scripture study. He said of the books of the Bible: "I wish that the plowman might sing parts of them at his plow and the weaver at his shuttle, and that the traveler might beguile with their narration the weariness of his way."

Through men inspired by his Spirit, God was directing attention to Bible study and to Bible translation. He was leading men to break the hard shell of tradition and custom which had almost smothered the gospel of Jesus Christ. He was directing attention to Greek as well as to Latin versions of the New Testament. He was guiding the minds of inventors.

Which of the men mentioned in this chapter would you like to honor in another marker on this long trail down which the Bible has come to us?

Perhaps you especially remember these eight:

> Erasmus
> Martin Luther
> Johann Gutenberg
> John Wycliffe
> King Alfred of England
> Aldhelm
> Bede
> Caedmon

No tablet would be large enough for names of all the people whom God used in these long-ago years of Bible preservation, Bible study, Bible translation, and Bible production.

Perhaps the inscription on one marker might read:

> *To John Wycliffe*
> *And other ancient men,*
> *Inspired of God*
> *To study and to sing,*
>
> *To preach and to write,*
> *To invent and to translate,*
> *That people might have the gospel*
> *In the English language.*

14

Men Who Dared to Think

Oxford, in England, is a sleepy little town, but in it is a great university which has been famous for more than seven hundred years. In that school, great teachers have often stirred the minds of young men, and there, in the year 1510, young William Tyndale was a student.

All over the world, the minds of men were beginning to wake up. Gutenberg's simple method of printing made more books available, and men discovered that thinking is exciting!

English printers began to use the new method, and more books appeared in the English language.

Persecuted Jewish scholars from Constantinople, Spain, and Portugal, had shared the wisdom of ancient cultures, and the printing of books in the Hebrew language began.

Columbus had set out to find a new route to India, and discovered America.

Oxford University today honors Tyndale as "the Apostle of England."

Copernicus studied mathematics and astronomy, and decided that the sun, and not the earth, is the center of the universe.

At Oxford University, William Tyndale continued to study and to think about many things, especially the Bible.

After he completed his work at Oxford, Tyndale went to Cambridge University. Later he was ordained a priest.

William Tyndale kept on studying and thinking. More and more, he realized that people need a Bible in a language they can read.

"I perceived by experience," Tyndale said, "that it was impossible to establish . . . people in any truth, unless the Scriptures are plainly laid before their eyes in their own language, so that they can see the process, order, and meaning of the text."

And William Tyndale had a big thought. He put it into words one day when a man protested that the Bible was only for highly educated people.

"If God spare my life, ere many years I will cause that the boy that driveth the plow shall know more of the Scripture than thou dost."

A farm boy read the Bible! The idea was unheard-of. Usually a day laborer could not even read English, much less Greek or Latin. Wycliffe's handwritten English Testament was expensive; and besides, it had been banned by both the Catholic Church and the English Government.

Yet Tyndale's big thought persisted. Soon he set to work to translate the Bible into English. He would begin with the New Testament, he decided, and because the New Testament had originally been written in Greek, he consulted copies of old Greek manuscripts as well as the newer Latin translations.

Would the Bishop of London approve his project? William Tyndale wondered about that, and made a trip to London to find out. A year of investigation convinced him that both Church and State would oppose him and that no printer would dare put an English manuscript of the Bible into type.

Yet, Tyndale reasoned, changes had come in Germany. And German printers might be more daring than English ones. Sadly, he left his beloved England for Germany, and there completed his translation of the New Testament into English.

Search for a brave printer began. At last one was found in Cologne, and immediately the job of setting type for an English New Testament began. In spite of Gutenberg's invention, the work was slow, for all type had to be set by hand.

Enemies of Bible translation discovered what was being done and persuaded the Government of Cologne to stop the printing. Tyndale escaped arrest and fled to the city of Worms.

He carried a precious bundle with him—three thousand sheets of his English New Testament which had already been printed.

In 1525, the first complete edition of the New Testament ever printed in the English language appeared in the city of Worms, Germany.

"How can I get these books into England?" Tyndale wondered, for he knew the officials would never allow their entrance if they knew about it.

Tyndale liked to go to fairs, and there he had met merchants who exported goods to England. He bargained with some of these men to hide New Testaments in sacks of grain, bundles of cloth, bales of fur, and other merchandise. Soon the shipments reached English ports.

"New Testaments printed in the English language are in this country!" The news spread throughout Britain.

Immediately there was a great demand for these books.

The people of England wanted to read them, and the Church leaders wanted to burn them!

An old record tells of a conversation between the Bishop of London and a merchant named Augustine Packington. The Bishop was seeking the English New Testament, and the merchant assured him that he could furnish many of the new books if the Bishop would pay the price.

The Bishop agreed.

"Do your diligence and get them, and with all my heart I will pay for them, whatsoever they cost you; for the books are erroneous and naughty, and I intend surely to destroy them all, and to burn them at Paul's Cross."

The merchant was a friend of William Tyndale. He reported the offer to Tyndale in Germany.

"William," he said, "I know thou art a poor man, and hast a heap of New Testaments and books by thee, for the which thou has both endangered thy friends and beggared thyself; and I have now gotten thee a merchant, which with ready money shall dispatch thee of all that thou hast."

"Who is the merchant?" asked Tyndale.

"The Bishop of London," replied Packington.

"He will burn them," Tyndale protested.

"Yes," agreed the merchant.

Tyndale thought for a moment.

"I am the gladder," he declared at last. "Two benefits

shall come thereof: I shall get money of him for these books, to bring myself out of debt, and the whole world shall cry out upon the burning of God's Word. . . . The money, that shall remain to me, shall make me more studious to correct the said New Testament, and so newly to imprint the same once again."

"And so," says the report, "forward went the bargain: the Bishop had the books, Packington had the thanks, and Tyndale had the money."

Events happened as Tyndale had known they would.

The English people were shocked at the burning of New Testaments; they clamored for those that remained. When they could not get complete ones, they bought a few pages.

And English New Testaments continued to be printed as Tyndale had planned.

Yet so successful was the effort to destroy these books that, of the edition begun at Cologne and completed at Worms, there is today known just one thirty-one-page fragment. Tyndale had carried eight of these pages with him when he fled from Cologne.

A copy of a later edition of Tyndale's New Testament, perfect except for one page, is now preserved in the Baptist College at Bristol, England. Another copy, lacking many pages, is in the library of St. Paul's, in London. Of the estimated eighteen thousand copies of Tyndale's New Testament printed at Worms, only these two have been found.

Still in Germany, Tyndale began to translate the Old Testament from Hebrew into English. Later he traveled to Belgium and carried on his work in Antwerp.

And in England, church authorities were at last convinced that the people were determined to read the Bible for themselves. They began to plan a translation of their own!

Yet these men continued their fierce attacks upon William Tyndale and his work. They charged that he objected to the "worship of images and relics, praying to saints and going on pilgrimage," much as Luther had done.

Tyndale's New Testament was a counterfeit, they said. It was full of errors. They protested at his translation of certain words. Tyndale's translation used "congregation" rather than "church," "elder" instead of "priest," "repent" instead of "do penance," and "love" instead of "charity."

Some of these criticisms were undoubtedly true, for Tyndale himself continued to work to improve his translation of the New Testament into English.

Yet, says one scholarly professor of our own time, "Tyndale's honesty, sincerity, and scrupulous integrity, his simple directness, his magical simplicity of phrase, his modest music, have given an authority to his wording that has imposed itself on all later versions of the Bible."

In Antwerp, Tyndale continued work on his translation of the Old Testament from Hebrew into English.

In the meantime, England, for political reasons, had

passed an act declaring the king, and not the pope, "the only supreme head on earth of the Church of England." There was, at this time, no change in church doctrine or attitudes toward the Bible, and opposition to Tyndale's teachings and work was so bitter and intense that it reached out even to Antwerp.

There Tyndale was betrayed by a man who pretended to be his friend. He was kidnapped in 1535 and thrown into a dungeon in Vilvorde Castle, near Brussels.

Yet, even in prison, he continued to study and to work on his translation of the Old Testament.

There he also wrote letters. One, written in Latin to an official of the government, has been translated into English. A part of it reads:

> I beg your lordship, and that by the Lord Jesus,
> That if I am to remain here through the winter,
> You will request the commissary
> To have the kindness to send me,
> From the goods of mine which he has,
> A warmer cap; . . . a warmer coat; . . .
> A piece of cloth to patch my leggings.
> My overcoat is worn out;
> My shirts are also worn out.
> He has a woollen shirt,
> If he will be good enough to send it. . . .
> And I ask to be allowed to have a lamp in the eve-
> ning. . . .
> But most of all I beg and beseech your clemency
> To be urgent with the commissary,

That he will kindly permit me to have the Hebrew
  Bible,
Hebrew grammar, and Hebrew dictionary,
That I may pass the time in that study. . . .
If any other decision has been taken concerning
  me, . . .
I will be patient, abiding the will of God,
To the glory of the grace of my Lord Jesus Christ.

The letter includes not one word of bitterness.

In August, 1536, Tyndale was brought to trial and declared guilty of holding and teaching false beliefs. He was put out of the priesthood and a sentence of death pronounced. His body was ordered burned.

Three months later the Vilvorde Prison doors opened and William Tyndale walked out into the sunlight.

Head up, the brave translator followed his guards to the public square. There he was tied to the stake. Then he spoke, and his words were a prayer,

"Lord, open the King of England's eyes."

Even as the flames shut his body from sight, William Tyndale's prayer was being answered.

Fires of truth were spreading throughout Great Britain, and a version of the Bible in the English language was being circulated. It did not bear Tyndale's name, but the translation was taken largely from his work. The Book was distributed with the permission of King Henry, who had come to the throne some years before.

Tyndale's big thought was becoming a reality. Soon

there would be a day when even a plowboy might read the Bible in the English language.

In 1535 another English translation of the Bible appeared, bearing the name of Myles Coverdale as translator. He had been Tyndale's friend, and this edition of the Bible was largely Tyndale's work.

Three years later a Bible in the English language was ordered "set up in a convenient place" in every church in Great Britain. To keep it from being carried away, it was usually chained to a reading desk.

People crowded about the desk to read God's Word in their own language. They even read during the sermons.

The Bible they read was made up of translations by Tyndale and Coverdale. Because of its size, it was called the "Great Bible." Some present-day Bibles still use words from this edition. Anyone who says "trespasses" rather than "debts" in the Lord's Prayer is quoting from the "Great Bible."

The Geneva Bible, although not authorized by the government, was important in the history of the English Scriptures. This version was prepared by men exiled from England during the rule of Catholic Queen Mary. The Geneva Version, made in Switzerland and dedicated to Queen Elizabeth, divided passages into verses. Both John Bunyan and John Knox used this edition, and the Puritans brought the Geneva translation to America.

In 1558 Elizabeth I became queen of England. At her coronation, in accordance with the custom of that time, petitions were made for the release of political prisoners.

One man presented a plea for five other men "long and unjustly detained in prison." His petition named them— "the four Evangelists and the Apostle Paul."

It declared that these five had "long been shut up in an unknown tongue, so that they could not converse with the common people."

The petition was not granted, but translations of the Bible continued to be made and printed without royal approval.

James I became king of England in 1603. In an effort to settle conflicting political and religious differences, a

Puritan leader proposed a new translation or revision of the Bible that would be acceptable to all groups.

King James appointed fifty-four scholars to undertake the work. They consulted Latin revisions and the English translations which had reflected so much of Tyndale's work; also a few other translations from the Greek.

Even as they were working, the Douay English Version, a translation from the Latin, was issued with the sanction of the Catholic Church. It was extremely literal. The translators said, "We presume not in hard places to mollify the speeches or phrases, but religiously keep them word for word."

In 1611 the first King James Version of the Bible appeared. The Preface said it was "translated out of the original tongues, and with former translations diligently compared and revised, by His Majesty's special command."

Yet even this edition was revised. Obsolete spelling was changed and various misprints corrected.

It was not until 1769 that the present form of the King James Version (known in England as the "Authorized Version") appeared. It has been called "the most beautiful Book in the world, in any language, a Book which has exercised an incalculable influence upon religion, upon manners, upon literature, and upon character."

This version has had wide circulation among English-speaking people all over the world. The plowboy has access to it, as Tyndale had hoped. Writers of the Gospels and the Epistles are no longer "imprisoned in a strange language."

Most English-speaking Christians are familiar with the King James Version of the Bible. For more than three hundred years, God has been speaking through it, and multitudes have understood his message.

A painting of William Tyndale hangs today in the great university he once attended in Oxford, England. Under it is a Latin inscription. Translated, a part of it reads:

> This likeness represents . . . William Tyndale,
> Formerly student and pride of this Hall,
> Who after reaping here the happy first-fruits
> Of a purer faith,
> Devoted his energy . . . to the translation
> Of the New Testament and Pentateuch . . . :
> A work so beneficial to his English countrymen,
> That he is not undeservedly called the Apostle of
> England.

In gratitude for the devotion of William Tyndale and others like him, another tablet might be erected on the trail down which the Bible has come to us.

This tablet would honor all of the heroes who worked with God in many different ways to give us the Bible in our own English language.

What words would you choose for a marker in honor of these men?

Perhaps your inscription would read like this:

To William Tyndale
And other devout men
Of scholarship and integrity,
Who dared think new thoughts
And who gave their efforts, their time,
And sometimes their lives,
That God might speak to people
Through the English Bible.

15

The Oldest Scroll

Did it all begin with a boy and a goat? Some people say it did. Read what happened and decide for yourself.

In the hot sands near Ain Feshkha, Chief Abdullah of the Ta-amirah tribe of Arabs pitched his tent not far from the Dead Sea. There was a well of fresh water at Ain Feshkha, and his men and beasts were thirsty.

Young Muhammad Dib let down the bucket into the well and enjoyed a cool drink. Then he drew water for his goats. When they had drunk, he herded them together and drove them back into the hills to find whatever bits of grass they could. He was sleepy, and it was hard to keep his mind on goats.

"I must not lose one," he said to himself. "The chief would be very angry, and I might not get any supper tonight."

Dib counted the goats.

"One can't be gone," he said to himself. "I have watched them every moment."

Wide awake now, he counted again and found that one goat was indeed missing. Dib ran into the hills.

It was strange-looking country and, in spite of his anxiety, Dib found it hard to keep his mind on the lost goat. His keen eyes picked out the stones and the low sandy mounds. They even saw a dark spot between two large rocks.

It was a perfect target to show skill in hitting the mark.

Dib picked up a small stone and threw it with all his might. It vanished into the darkness, and Dib heard a sound like something breaking.

Startled, he began to run. Were there thieves hidden in those rocks? Dib almost stumbled over the lost goat on the way back to camp.

That night he thought for a long time about what had happened. He told his friend Musa about it.

They decided to explore the rocks next day.

"Maybe we'll find something that we can trade for some sweets in Bethlehem when the tribe gets there," Musa said.

"Or we could save the money and buy a camel of our own," Dib suggested.

Next morning the two boys made their way over the hot, dry sands, and soon Dib pointed to the hole where he had aimed his stone.

Musa drew back. "Are you sure you heard something break?" he asked.

"I am very sure," Dib said.

He peered into the blackness, but he could see nothing. Slowly, he began to inch his way through the narrow opening. He found it a bit wider as he went farther. At last he could stand up. Dib drew a long breath of the cool, dry air.

As his eyes grew accustomed to the darkness, he stared about him in amazement. For he saw that he was in a cave. About him stood rows and rows of tall jars. At his feet lay a broken jar and, beside it, the stone he had thrown into the cave.

He was picking up one of the fragments when he heard a movement by his side.

"I just couldn't wait any longer," Musa explained.

"Looks like we have only found a lot of old jars. They won't sell for much."

Dib nodded. "We might as well look at them since we're here," he said.

He lifted one of the jars and pushed back the lid. He coughed and stepped back, holding his nose. The dust and stench almost choked him.

Still Dib was curious. Cautiously he put his hand down into the jar and felt something hard. Slowly he pulled out a bundle wrapped in cloth and covered with a black, waxlike substance.

"What on earth is it?" asked Musa. He had pulled similar objects from other jars.

Dib shook his head. "I don't know," he said. "Let's take them outside and look at them."

Dib crept back through the black tunnel with a bundle in his hands. Musa followed with two more bundles.

"They must be old," Dib told his friend. "The bundles are wrapped in strips of cloth like mummies, and they smell terrible."

"Some people like old things," Musa said. He turned up his nose. "Maybe we can get a little something for these."

Dib was punching the bundle and pulling at what seemed to be a loose end.

"It's a scroll," he told Musa at last. "Once I saw one in a merchant's booth in Bethlehem. There is writing on it."

"Just a scroll!" Musa was disgusted.

"Let's show it to the sheik," Dib suggested. "If merchants sell them, they must buy them, too. Maybe we can get a little money for these."

The two boys lugged their three scrolls back to camp.

They approached the sheik and slapped each other's open palms.

The sheik returned their respectful greeting.

"Salaam," he said. "Peace to you. What have you brought?"

The tribesmen gathered around as the boys showed their bundles.

Sheik Abdullah unrolled the scrolls and agreed that they seemed quite old. He broke off a bit of one scroll and looked at the writing on it. He shook his head.

"I cannot read these words," he said at last. "They are not in our Arabic language. I think they are Syrian."

"Some of the merchants in Bethlehem read that language," a tribesman said.

The sheik agreed.

"We'll see what we can find out," he told Dib and Musa.

He ordered a camel loaded with cheese and watermelons, and chose several goats and sheep to sell. The three set out at once for Bethlehem, carrying the three scrolls with them. They must travel in the coolness of night, for the heat of the sun made daytime traveling impossible at that time of year.

In Bethlehem, Sheik Abdullah sold his goats and his sheep, his cheese and watermelons. Then he set out to find a Syrian merchant who, he knew, often sold old things.

The two men sipped sweet tea from tall glasses in a cafe and Sheik Abdullah told of the finding of the scrolls.

"They are very valuable," he assured the merchant.

"How do you know?" the merchant asked.

The sheik could not answer that question, but he unrolled one of the scrolls.

As he did so, a piece broke, and the merchant examined it. He saw that the scroll was actually two strips of leather sewn together, making one long narrow strip. He looked at the writing and shook his head.

"I cannot read it," he admitted. "The scrolls may be old, and the writing ancient Syrian."

"What will you give for them?" the sheik asked.

The Syrian waited a moment.

"Come back next week," he suggested. "Leave the scrolls here and I will think about them." He did not tell the sheik that he wished to show them to another merchant who knew more about such things.

Sheik Abdullah handed over a bundle and went back to the camels.

Dib and Musa saw him coming and noticed that he carried no bundle.

"Did you get a good price for the scrolls?" they asked.

Sheik Abdullah shook his head.

"I could not sell them," he told the boys, "but the

merchant is interested. You may look for more scrolls this week if you wish."

The boys were quiet as they returned to camp.

Next day Dib had to promise his knife to Musa before he would go again to the cave with him.

Another tribesman went with them this time. The boys brought back two scrolls and the tribesman brought three.

Several weeks later they went with the sheik to Bethlehem.

The merchant there did not tell Sheik Abdullah that he had made a trip to Jerusalem, and had showed a scroll to a merchant there. One had also been left at the Syrian Orthodox Monastery with Archbishop Samuel, who had seemed interested.

The merchant in Bethlehem did give the sheik a note to George Isaiah, the merchant in Jerusalem.

The four Arabs went on to Jerusalem.

George Isaiah told them something of his visit to the Syrian Monastery of St. Mark, and took them there. With them, the men carried seven scrolls. Isaiah had kept two with him. The Archbishop had one.

At the monastery gate they showed their scrolls. The priest on duty held his nose.

"This is a Syrian monastery," he shouted. "We are not interested in Hebrew."

"The Archbishop told me to come," Isaiah protested.

The gatekeeper slammed the gate.

"I shall sell my scrolls to someone else," the tribesman said. Off he went with his two scrolls.

Silently Dib and Musa followed the sheik and Isaiah down the narrow street.

"The Archbishop told me the scrolls were written in Hebrew," Isaiah explained to the sheik. "Yet he seemed interested in buying them."

Sheik Abdullah thought for a moment.

"Hebrew is the old language of the Jews," he said. "Maybe we can sell the scrolls to the Jews."

It was wartime, and Isaiah had many things on his mind. But he gave the sheik the name of a Jewish merchant at the Jaffa Gate.

The merchant agreed to buy the scrolls.

"Come to my office in the Jaffa Road in an hour and I will pay you," he promised.

The sheik agreed.

In the Syrian monastery, Bishop Samuel paced the floor. He had had a telephone call from Bethlehem that morning, saying the scrolls were on their way to Jerusalem. He had studied the one left with him and had decided to buy it. He waited impatiently. At last he went to the gatekeeper.

"Let me know when some Arabs arrive," he ordered. "I want to see them as soon as they get here."

The gatekeeper stared in amazement. "They were here this morning," he admitted. "I sent them away."

"Why?" the Archbishop demanded.

"They were dirty, and carried worthless Hebrew scrolls with them. The odor was bad, and I knew our monastery was only interested in the Syrian language."

Nobody knows exactly what the Archbishop said first.

"Telephone George Isaiah, the Syrian merchant," he ordered when he had thought for a time. "Let me talk with him."

Luckily the telephone was working, and George Isaiah could be reached.

Archbishop Samuel expressed his regret at what had happened. "I will purchase the scrolls," he said. "Can you return with the Arabs today?"

At once Isaiah set out to search for Sheik Abdullah. He found him and the two boys at the Jaffa Gate.

"You haven't sold the scrolls, have you?" he panted.

Abdullah explained that he was to go to the Jewish dealer's office on the Jaffa Road for his money.

Isaiah thought fast. He must prevent that, if he were to have a part in the sale.

"The Jaffa Road is dangerous," he told the sheik, "especially for Arabs. You must remember that the Jews and the Arabs are still at war. Someone might steal the scrolls from you. You might even be killed."

Sheik Abdullah knew that there was still fighting in the city. He had heard of strange and terrible things happening to Arabs in Jerusalem.

He looked at the two boys. At last he agreed to go back to the monastery.

This time Isaiah went with them.

Archbishop Samuel bought their five scrolls and also the one in his possession. The amount he paid was about a hundred and fifty dollars.

Dib promised to take the Archbishop to see the cave where the scrolls had been found, and the Arabs went back to camp happy with their bargain.

The Archbishop came a few days later. Dib showed him the cave, and the camel he had bought with his share of the money.

This is almost the end of the story of Dib and his goats, but you cannot yet answer the question with which this chapter started.

Did it all begin with a boy and a goat? Read the rest of this chapter before you decide.

For the story of the Dead Sea Scrolls continues.

It leads again to the Syrian monastery in Jerusalem, where Archbishop Samuel continued to study the scrolls. He showed them to all his visitors.

One of these, said to be an authority on such matters, was quite positive in his opinion.

"The scrolls are fakes," he declared.

Still Archbishop Samuel believed them to be genuine.

One day he showed them to a Dutch Bible scholar who was also a Hebrew scholar.

"They were found near Ain Feshkha," he said.

"There is nothing in that region," the scholar said.

Yet he examined one scroll. He felt the parchment and

looked at it carefully for a long time. He smelled it. He studied the writing with a magnifying glass.

At last he looked up at Archbishop Samuel and spoke.

"This seems to be a manuscript of the book of Isaiah," he said. "I do not know how old it is, but I believe we are looking at the oldest book of Isaiah now in existence."

Professors and other scholars in Jerusalem could not believe his report.

At last news of the scrolls reached the head of the American School of Oriental Research, in Jerusalem. Dr. John Trever, an American, went to the monastery. He examined the scrolls and was convinced that they are ancient. He secured permission to have them photographed.

War was still going on, and the lights went off several times during the photographing process, but at last prints of the Isaiah Scroll were sent to an outstanding archaeologist in America. He examined them and immediately sent a report to Jerusalem by air mail.

My heartiest congratulations on the greatest manuscript discovery of modern times! There is no doubt in my mind that the script is . . . around 100 B.C. . . . There can happily not be the slightest doubt in the world about the genuineness of the manuscript!

On May 15, 1948, British government came to an end in Palestine. Israel was declared an independent state. Again the Jewish people were a free nation.

Representatives of the Government of Israel met formally several months later.

In that group were men who had come from concentration camps and ghettos. It included men who had seen their families tortured. Some had seen relatives sent to gas chambers on no charge except that they were Jews. Many of those men bore on their own bodies marks of persecution for the same reason.

On his desk, each representative of Israel found a report of the finding of the Dead Sea Scrolls. He also found a photograph of the fortieth chapter of Isaiah, made from those same scrolls.

In the ancient language of his people, each man read words that you can find in your Bible. He read words beginning:

> Comfort ye,
> Comfort ye my people,
> Saith your God.

The story of the Dead Sea Scrolls is not quite finished.

Dr. Trever went to the monastery and was told that they were no longer there. Where they were at that time is a mystery.

Those same scrolls appeared in America in January, 1949, along with the old Archbishop. They were safe!

No one seems to know exactly how, but at last the Dead Sea Scrolls were brought together. At one time they were advertised for sale in an American newspaper.

They were sold in 1954 to the state of Israel for two hundred and fifty thousand dollars.

Today Israel is known as "the Land of the Book." And there, in the Hebrew University in Jerusalem, the Isaiah Scrolls rest.

Translators have found their words little different from the book of Isaiah which you read in your Bible. The message is the same.

Examination of other Dead Sea Scrolls goes on, but it is a slow process. Those made of leather must be softened in a moist glass case and brushed with oil and handled carefully to prevent crumbling.

Some of the scrolls are made of copper, and these have to be treated by a special process before they can be unrolled and studied.

It may be beyond the year 2000 before the translation of the Dead Sea Scrolls is completed.

Yet the work continues to add to our understanding of the Bible and how it came to us.

It would be hard to plan a marker to include all the people who had a part in the discovery of the Dead Sea Scrolls. How many can you think of? Would your list include a boy with God-given curiosity?

Would it name Sheik Abdullah, Archbishop Samuel, and Dr. John Trever?

How about archaeologists and other scholars with disciplined minds who worked with persistence and intelligence?

Would you include careful copyists and men of faith who wrapped the scrolls carefully and stored them away more than two thousand years ago?

How about scientists and translators who continue to study old manuscripts?

You could not mention all of these people on a marker on the Bible trail. Yet you would think of them as you chose an inscription something like this:

This marker is dedicated
To boys with inquisitive minds
And to men of patience and skill
Who labored with devotion
To produce and preserve
Our oldest copy of a Bible book.

16

God's Continuing Message

What has an old Hebrew manuscript of Isaiah to do with my English Bible?

To answer that question, we must look at some of the ways the discoveries of archaeologists and scientists influence books and their translation.

Do you remember the story of the Gezer Calendar and how men learned more about the Hebrew language and word meanings from it? That calendar was an archaeological discovery that enabled scholars to understand better what old languages mean. Such discoveries continue to be made. They continue to help us understand long-ago customs and languages.

In this same way, the Isaiah Scroll helps. No original scroll of a book of the Bible has yet been discovered. The Dead Sea Scroll of Isaiah is more than nine centuries older than any yet found. Yet it confirms the message of Isaiah which you read in your English Bible.

Others of those Dead Sea Scrolls throw light on customs mentioned in your Bible.

All of them point to the preservation of the Book which God inspired men to write.

How do we know the Dead Sea Scroll of Isaiah is more than two thousand years old? You would need to read many books to answer that question fully.

Studying the way a manuscript is written helps to determine its age. How are the letters formed? When did people write like that? Are the letters joined together? Are the words separated from each other? This study of handwriting is called paleography. Careful paleographers helped to determine the age of the Dead Sea Scrolls.

An analysis of the ink with which the manuscripts were written was made. Long-ago ink contained no iron. The analysis of ink from the Dead Sea Scrolls helped to determine the date of their writing.

One of the newest fields of science helped in the study of the scrolls. The use of Carbon 14 grew out of our atomic energy research. By burning a piece of material made from a plant and analyzing the ashes, scientists are able to tell approximately how long ago the plant was alive. Scientists burned a bit of the old linen in which the scrolls of Isaiah were wrapped. An analysis of the ashes revealed that the linen was made from flax which grew more than a hundred years before Jesus was born.

The study of words, too, helps to determine the age of any manuscript. For, through the years, words change in meaning. Unless people can read the Bible in words of their own times, they find it very difficult to understand its meaning.

Have you ever had an examination to determine what help your eyes need, to do their job well? If so, you remember the chart which the doctor shows you.

"Read the first line," he says.

"Now read the second.

"Try the third."

At last the doctor asks, "How many lines on the chart can you read?"

Your answer tells something of your eyes' strength or weakness.

Let's look at another kind of chart, a chart which may help you to understand why old truths must often be put into new words. This might be called an Understanding Chart.

Here are three lines from English Bibles:

"Vren hlaf ofer wirthe sel us to daeg."

"Give to us this dai oure breed ouer other substance."

"Give us this day our daily bread."

Did you understand the first line?
How about the second one?
Which line did you understand best?
The first of these lines was from an English Bible published about A.D. 900. The second was from an English Bible of 1382; the third, from a version published several years ago.

From these lines, you can tell something about changes in the spelling and meaning of words through the years.

"God's truth does not change," you may be saying. And you are right. Yet words do change in both spelling and meaning. You can hear God speaking through the Bible only to the degree that you understand what its words mean today.

Let's try another experiment on the best-loved version of the English Bible, the King James Version. This, you remember, was first published in 1611. Here are six verses from my King James Version of the Bible:

"Surely there is a vein for the silver,
    And a place for gold where they fine it"

(Job 28:1).

"Only let your conversation be
as it becometh the gospel of Christ"
(Philippians 1:27).

"If there be therefore any consolation
in Christ, if any comfort of love, if any fellowship
of the Spirit, if any bowels and mercies,
fulfil ye my joy, that ye be likeminded"
(Philippians 2:1).

"All scripture is given by inspiration of God . . .
that the man of God may be perfect, throughly
furnished unto all good works"
(2 Timothy 3:16–17).

"Suffer little children, and forbid them not,
to come unto me:
for of such is the kingdom of heaven"
(Matthew 19:14).

"Thou, Lord, hast holpen me"
(Psalm 86:17).

How well did you understand those verses? In each
one, did you find at least one word used in a way
unfamiliar to you, or spelled in a way that seems strange?

Look at this list which gives the meanings of some old
words as they are used in these verses. Then test what you
thought each verse meant:

Fine—refine
Conversation—manner of life
Bowels—warm affection
Throughly—thoroughly
Furnished—equipped
Suffer—allow
Holpen—helped

Did some of the meanings surprise you?

Look at these same verses in later versions of the Bible and decide whether the older or newer versions best help you to understand God's message which he has given in his Book.

The versions quoted are the Revised Standard Version [RSV], the New English Bible [NEB], Montgomery, and American Standard Version [ASV].

"Surely there is a mine for silver,
    and a place for gold which they refine."   RSV

"Only let your conduct be worthy of the gospel of
    Christ."   NEB

"If then our common life in Christ yields anything
    to stir the heart,
    any loving compassion, any sharing of the Spirit,
    any warmth of affection or compassion, fill up my
    cup of happiness by thinking and feeling alike." NEB

"All scripture is inspired of God . . .
that the man of God may be complete,
equipped for every good work." RSV

"Let the little children come to me, and forbid
them not; for it is to the childlike that the kingdom
of heaven belongs." Montgomery

"Thou, Jehovah, hast helped me." ASV

Do you think we frequently need present-day words to help us understand the Bible?

On my bookshelf I have more than a dozen different kinds of English Bibles. One, of course, is the King James Version, which I have had for many years. Another revision was made in America in 1901. This was the edition studied by most of our older ministers.

The Revised Standard Version, published in 1952, was made by scholars representing Christians of many faiths.

One edition is a translation by Helen Barrett Montgomery. This is, as far as I know, the only translation made by a woman.

A very readable edition of the New Testament is that of J. B. Phillips, made in England a few years ago. An older version was translated by James Moffatt. Another American translation was made by Dr. Edgar Goodspeed. One translation of the New Testament bears the name of

Charles B. Williams as translator. Another volume does not bear the name of the translator.

In all of these versions, the wording is different.

Yet, not one changes a basic teaching of the Bible.

In all these versions, God is speaking. He is calling us to faith in his Son. In all of them, he is calling us to a life of faith that follows the example of our Lord.

As I write, two new translations of the Old Testament are being made in England. The Jewish people have published a new translation of the Torah—the books of the Law. Catholics are revising the Douay Version of the Bible.

More and more versions will come. And through all of these, God will be speaking to those who seek him.

Before the Bible, there was God,
And there were people.
Because he loved people,
God was always reaching out to them.

In the long ago, God inspired good men
To make written records
Of truths about him.
They wrote the books that make up our Bible.

Hundreds of years later
God put into the hearts of other men
The impulse to translate the Bible
Into languages people could understand.

Today God speaks through the Bible
In more than a thousand languages,
And in every language,
The message is the same.

"God loves you," the Bible says.
"Because he loves you, he sent his Son.
The Father sent the Son
To be the Saviour of the world."

Words change in meaning,
But God's truth is always the same,
And through the Bible
God is still speaking.

In the Bible God is speaking to you and to me
And inviting us to fellowship with him.